On the Shoulders

of Giants

by

Craig Loehle

GEORGE RONALD

OXFORD

GEORGE RONALD, Publisher
46 High Street, Kidlington, Oxford OX5 2DN

© CRAIG LOEHLE 1994
All Rights Reserved

ISBN 0-85398-362-3

*A Cataloguing-in-Publication entry is available
from the British Library*

Contents

Acknowledgements   vi

Introduction   1

**1. Race: A Combined Scientific and
Spiritual Perspective**   9

  Scientific Approaches   10
    The Biology of Race   10
    Race and Culture   14
    The Biology of Racism   17
    The Ecology of Cultural Advance   23
  Spiritual Approaches   33
  Conclusion   39

2. Spiritual Synergy for a New Ecology   40

  Introduction   40
  Spiritual Disharmonies   42
    Connections with Nature   42
    Reverence   46
    A Short-Term Perspective   49
  Practical Steps   57
    War and the Environment   58
    Prejudice   60
    The Status of Women   63
  Conclusion: Spiritual Synergy   67

3. **Creativity: The Divine Gift**   68

    Introduction   68
    The Creative Act   70
    Hubris and Humility   71
    Detachment   78
    Tranquillity   81
    Honesty   85
    Service   88
    Science as a Calling   90
    Conclusion   90

4. **Evolution in Bahá'í Perspective**   92

    Introduction   93
    Science and God's Existence   98
    Human Evolution   104

5. **Knowledge and Faith**   116

6. **Growth and Stability of the Bahá'í Administrative Order: Lessons from Biology**   128

    Growth   128
    Stability   136

7. **Entropy and the Integrity of the Sacred Texts**   145

    Message Transmission and Parables   150
    Safeguards of Meaning in the Bahá'í Sacred Writings   153

8. **Probability and Prophecy**   163

9. **God Under the Microscope**   176

    Traditional Arguments and the
      Nature of Evidence   177
    New Arguments for God's
      Existence   181
      Predictive Power   181
      Theory Coherence   183
      Consilience   187
    Conclusion   190

Bibliography   191

References   197

Acknowledgements

I attribute the initial impetus to begin writing on Bahá'í subjects to conversations and letters from the late Dr Magdalene Carney who encouraged me over a five-year period. Dr Janet Khan also helped me to use my scientific training in service to the Bahá'í Faith and encouraged me considerably. I must also mention encouragement and support I received from Dr Peter Khan and Sue Fouts. Helpful comments have been provided by Lawrence Arturo, Todd Ewing, Peter Haug, Jolie Haug, Sharon Hepp, Peyvand Khademi, Audrey Lindau, Marcia Le Roy, Frank Lewis, Thomas Payton, David Schlesinger, Luther Smith, Robert Stockman, Patricia West, Truitt White, and reviewers of the *Journal of Bahá'í Studies* and *World Order* magazine.

Permission to reprint 'Evolution in Bahá'í Perspective' has been kindly granted by the Association for Bahá'í Studies in whose *Journal* it appeared in April 1990 under the title of 'On Human Origins: A Bahá'í Perspective'. A short version of this article appeared in *Herald of the South*, January–March 1993. A short version of the article entitled 'Race: A Combined Scientific and Spiritual Perspective' appeared in *Herald of the South* in October 1993.

I dedicate this book to my wife and children, but especially to Bahá'u'lláh, without whom I would not be the person I am today.

Introduction

Newton is famous for his statement that if he had seen farther than others it was because he stood on the shoulders of giants. The theme of this book is the same: what might we see when our perspective is elevated about the normal day-to-day view. But whereas Newton stood on the shoulders of giants of science such as Kepler and Galileo, I have in mind a slightly different metaphor. I imagine two sets of shoulders: one set is Newton's, who represents science and technology, and the other is Bahá'u'lláh's, who represents the world of religion and divine guidance. For the first time in history, in the Bahá'í Faith we have been given the assurance that science and religion must not only agree but are in fact compatible and harmonious. In the past science 'agreed' with religion but at the expense of the integrity of science. This led to considerable conflict between the two as science began to mature after Galileo. The harmony of science and religion proclaimed by Bahá'u'lláh, and being put into practice by Bahá'ís, is of a deeper sort than a mere truce or an agreement to have jurisdictions over separate domains of knowledge. This harmony arises from a deep-rooted, fundamental coincidence of world views and of the ways that we go about achieving understanding and knowledge. This book explores what new perspective may be gained from standing with one foot in each world – one foot on the shoulder of each giant, each domain of knowledge – and see what insights may be gained thereby.

In the history of science it has often been observed that the cross-fertilization between two fields leads to an explosion of knowledge. For example, geometry and algebra had been developed centuries before Galileo but had been used only for describing shapes. Galileo showed that they could be used to describe the motion of objects such as heavy balls rolling down inclines, thereby opening the door to all of modern physics. The development of physics led to new mathematics such as the calculus, and so on in a continuing feedback cycle of mutual development. It is exactly this kind of mutual benefit and reinforcement that I see latent in the potential interactions between science and religion.

In the modern world we are very proud of our technology, and justifiably so, but we now find ourselves torn loose from our moorings, bouncing about helplessly inside the juggernaut of our high-tech society. We have no sense of place or of history. We have lost touch with the land. Modern corporations have little loyalty to their employees and demand more and more from them. We witness a rampant individualism that has almost destroyed any sense of community or of mutual obligation to each other. We have made a Faustian deal, indeed.

Similarly, religion is adrift. Mainstream religions are losing membership. Fundamentalist denominations are growing by appealing to emotionalism and the search for certainty which rigid absolutism brings. Neither group has much impact on the life of society. For many educated people, religion has lost its validity, and if they attend church at all, it is for social reasons alone. The reason, of course, is that religion (as espoused by the more fundamental), asks that one believe twelve impossible things before breakfast. It is difficult for modern, educated people to resist doubt under these conditions.

Thus it is clear that the two pillars of society, technology and religion, are seriously wounded, bleeding, and in need of a transfusion. This book seeks to begin the infusion of fresh blood into these domains via a mutual exchange of vital essence between the two.

Before beginning briefly to set the stage for the discussion to follow, it is helpful to provide a panoramic overview of the Bahá'í Faith for those who may not be familiar with it. The Bahá'í Faith began in 1844 when the Báb (which means the Gate) declared that He was the Promised One of Islam. His ministry was brief and dramatic, calling to mind that of Christ. In fact, the parallels are many, including His short ministry, His confrontation with the authorities and His final martyrdom by firing squad in 1850, a martyrdom accompanied by a darkening of the sky and an earthquake, among other miraculous events. The persecution of His followers, of whom 20,000 gave their lives, directly parallels in both intensity and cruelty the slaughter of the early Christians by the Romans. The Báb, however, said that He was preparing the way for an even greater teacher who would follow Him. In 1863 Bahá'u'lláh (whose name means the Glory of God) declared that He was this teacher, sent to educate all humankind. Since that time the Bahá'í Faith has spread very rapidly, within its first century penetrating every corner of the globe.

Essentially, the Bahá'í Faith is about renewal, fulfilment and evolution. In all of these traits it asserts a universal character and makes profound spiritual claims. These central themes are what is unique and compelling about it, not the particular teachings it propounds such as the equality of men and women, attractive as these may be. A collection of nice principles is not a religion and it was not for such ideals that the early Bahá'ís gave their lives or that thousands since then have spread out to every corner of the globe to share its message. There is something deeper involved.

While the teachings brought by the prophets do not become outdated, the religions by which those teachings are manifested are subject to decay just as is any physical order. People add rituals, comment on the texts in contradictory ways, change the meanings of words, and change the emphasis of the religion until eventually it is barely recognizable and ceases to guide and inspire. Christianity has fragmented to the point that it is hard to call it a single religion anymore. Some churches wait for the Advent and expect the Rapture. Others say this will never occur, that it is only symbolic. Some cater mainly for the rich. Some handle snakes and speak in tongues. One church believes in the Trinity, one focuses exclusively on Jesus, and another views Him as merely a great historical figure. One sprinkles,

one dunks. One forbids dancing while another
dances in the aisles. One drinks wine in church while
another forbids drinking altogether. It is hard to
believe that all of these even derive from the same
source, much less that they are the same religion. In
addition to this fragmentation of belief and ritual, of
rules and customs, over time religious organizations
themselves become corrupted or rigid and out of
touch. It is therefore necessary, for many reasons,
for religion to be periodically renewed. Bahá'u'lláh
asserts that this is His purpose, and refers to this day
as the Divine Springtime. When God renews His
eternal faith, He sweeps away the cobwebs of superstition, man-made encrustations, outmoded rituals
and incorrect interpretations. The need for such renewal has never been greater because today people
are educated. Being thus enabled to learn about
corruption, to read the holy books for themselves,
and to witness contradictions, they become intolerant of what religion has become, and ultimately
become disillusioned. This is true of Islam as well as
of Christianity, of Hinduism as well as of Buddhism
because all of these, to a greater or lesser extent and
in diverse ways, suffer from this internal decay and
fragmentation and need renewal.

It is the Bahá'í belief, a belief borne out by history,
that such renewal cannot be accomplished by human
effort. Attempts to reform existing religions have
merely led to the formation of new sects and denominations in a seemingly endless proliferation. This
trend further increases with each passing day the confusion of the ordinary person concerning religion.
What is needed is a fresh infusion of the divine spirit,

brought by One who has the power to inspire and the authority to challenge existing institutions. Such a One, Bahá'ís believe, is Bahá'u'lláh.

In order to distinguish between a mere reformer or teacher and a true Prophet, which Bahá'u'lláh claims to be, we come to the second great theme of the Bahá'í Faith: fulfilment. It is a curious fact that in all the existing major world religions there is an expectation that a Great One will come. In every case this person is expected to be a universal teacher (i.e. One who will reach all humankind) and in each case the events associated most strongly with Him concern the establishment of world peace. The Christians await the Return. The Jews await the Messiah. The Zoroastrians await the Shah Bahram. The Buddhists await the Fifth (universal) Buddha. The Hindus await Kalki Avatar. In all cases this person is expected to end a universal cycle or historical age and inaugurate a new, unique period in human history. It is also promised that He will renew the pure essence of religion and restore it to greater glory than ever before, the idea of renewal mentioned above. Bahá'u'lláh claims to be this universal Manifestation: to the Christians He is the return of the spirit of Christ, the Comforter, the Counsellor, the Prince of Peace; to the Hindus He is Kalki Avatar, etc. Thus it is that Bahá'u'lláh is not an abrogator of past revelation, but a fulfiller. He has come not to destroy the faiths of the peoples, but to fulfil the potentials inherent in those faiths, until now unrevealed. Even more, He has come in specific fulfilment of promises and prophecies made in all the holy books. These prophecies are not all vague statements that someone will come someday. Many of them are quite specific, giving times, places and events said to surround His person when He appears. Bahá'ís have several books on this subject and one of the chapters in this book addresses some of the more specific promises made regarding the dates of Bahá'u'lláh's advent. We note also that the fulfilment of the promises concerning the great peace are fulfilled by Bahá'u'lláh, not in the form of a miracle, but in the form of a comprehensive set of teachings which will bring about this peace, teachings which neither singly nor together have ever before been propounded by a religious leader.

It has long been said in the holy books that there were more truths than humanity was ready to hear, but in this day these truths are revealed. Daniel was told that the books were sealed until the time of the end.[1] Christ said that there were many things He had to say, but the people could not yet bear to hear them; when the Comforter came, He would lead them unto all truth.[2] Similar statements appear in the other holy books.

This idea of untold truths that would be revealed at the time of the end leads us to the third great theme of the Bahá'í Faith: evolution. The fulfilment of the promises in the holy books requires that the new Prophet not only renew the pure spirit of religion, but reveal new truths that were hidden before. This implies that religion is capable of progress. We observe from historical enquiries that in fact over the last five thousand years religion has undergone considerable development in terms of theological concepts, ethical standards, and outward forms, among others. The promises in the extant holy books that there is yet more to be revealed implies that religion as we currently view it, and as currently manifested in books such as the Bible, is not the last and highest possible expression of God's word. Thus there is a higher level of development possible for religion, a level which Bahá'ís believe Bahá'u'lláh has revealed. We witness this in the revelation of many specific teachings appropriate for the modern world but which were not relevant or attainable in the past, such as the abolition of the priesthood, the equality of men and women and the abolition of slavery. One of the most important of these new teachings, and the focus of this book, is the harmony of science and religion. Such a teaching could not be revealed in the past because there was no such thing as science. Today, this teaching is absolutely necessary lest religion completely lose its credibility and science cause us to lose our humanity. Even more than this, if we can combine science and religion in a genuine partnership, we empower them to solve the problems that have bedevilled humanity for thousands of years. This book explores how this partnership may be put into practice, not in the abstract but in the realm of real problems and issues such as racism, the environment, human development and other pressing concerns. Conversely, I show how scientific concepts throw light on the processes of religion, including an examination of prophecy using probability theory and of parables using information theory.

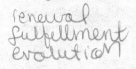

I

Race

A Combined Scientific and Spiritual Perspective

When an issue proves as intractable as race has over a prolonged period, it is clear that we are looking at it from the wrong perspective. We can now see that appeals to 'rights' and 'fairness' are inadequate to prevent a resurgence of racism in America. Nor will power politics, quotas or legislation eliminate the economic problems that exist. As an alternative, I would like to present a completely new perspective on race. Just as the astronauts brought back pictures of the whole Earth, pictures which forcefully brought home the fact that we are all very close together on a very small, fragile planet hurtling through the void, I would like to view race from a different angle and from a greater distance so that perhaps we can see the larger picture.

My objective is to examine race with a new eye, as though it were a newly discovered thing, using the dual perspectives of science and religion. Only by taking this dual perspective can we hope to resolve this tangled issue.

Scientific Approaches

The Biology of Race

When a biologist looks at a trait, one of the questions asked is the function of the trait. Some traits may be accidental, such as the exact pattern of colours in the peacock's tail, or non-adaptive, such as the vestigial human appendix; but for a trait such as human skin colour that is so uniform within a geographic region, we may be sure that there is some reason for it, that is, it has arisen over time due to natural selection (i.e. evolution).

What is the reason for skin colour differences? Skin colour across geographic regions varies as a result of a trade-off between sunburn and rickets. Humans evolved in Africa under a tropical sun, most likely on the savannas. Primitive humans, being without either fur or clothing, were strongly selected for dark skin colour to protect against the sun. The hippo, which is also hairless, avoids the sun by being nocturnal and submerging in the water by day. Elephants spend a lot of time in the shade and have thick, horny, dark grey skin to protect themselves. Humans have poor night vision, however, and must be active by day, so protection is essential. To gauge the extent of selective pressure, consider the fate of redheads left naked on the African grasslands. They would not only be so burned that they would be sun sick, under primitive conditions the severe cracking of the skin would probably lead to fatal infections. Furthermore, such a person if exposed to the sun every day for years would most likely get skin cancer by the age of 20. Conversely, a very dark person in a northern latitude is at a disadvantage with respect to vitamin D. In response to sunlight striking the skin, we all naturally produce vitamin D. In northern latitudes, however, where people spend a great deal of time indoors and are often covered by heavy clothing, sufficient vitamin D is not produced. Further, dark skins are less efficient at producing vitamin D. Lack of D leads to rickets, a severe deformity of the bones especially manifest as bow-leggedness. Before vitamin D was added to milk, northern Europeans feared rickets and made a point of taking their children out for sun, especially in winter. Under primitive conditions, therefore, very dark individuals would have been at a severe disadvantage in northern latitudes.

Thus from the standpoint of biology, both dark and light skin have adaptive significance. From the standpoint of racial differences, however, it seems that we are attributing undue significance to differences in susceptibility to sunburn and rickets. If we heard of a case of discrimination against people allergic to strawberries, it would certainly seem odd. If I said I make friends only with people who are highly susceptible to skin cancer, it would also seem odd, but that is in effect what racism is. In fact, with the current thinning of the ozone layer causing more ultraviolet light to reach the earth, increased skin pigment is a definite advantage.

Another thing that we may note about skin colour – it is a very superficial trait biologically. Those biological traits that are closely linked to functional aspects of our physiology tend to be uniform and resistant to change. All humans have the same DNA code, the same basic proteins, the same essential internal functioning. This is due to the recent origin of the various races from common ancestors.

When we trace our earliest ancestors back several million years, Africa appears to be the cradle of both ancient and modern forms.[1] While very primitive humans (*Homo erectus* and later Neanderthal) spread out from Africa to Europe and Asia over a million years ago, modern humans arose in Africa about 200,000 years ago.[2] About 100,000 years ago modern humans spread out from Africa in a great wave and supplanted preexisting early humans in Europe and Asia.[3] This date thus represents the beginning of the worldwide spread of humanity and the earliest date for racial differentiation. Such a comparatively recent origin for the races means that most racial differences are rather superficial and trivial.[4]

The very recent origin of the several races of humanity is important. Evolutionary change is very slow and over short intervals typically only external and superficial features such as skin colour, hair texture and ear shape have time to change. The differences between the races are largely of this superficial type. All the races can marry and produce viable offspring. We can all cross-donate blood and organs. The essential features that make us human are largely identical between the races. In fact, the mitochondrial DNA differences between races are only about 15% of the mean within-population variance.[5] That is, there are far more differences between the individuals within a race than there are between the average individuals of different races.

Men and women are more fundamentally different than are a black man and a white man. Men and women differ in life span, muscle mass, bone density, skull thickness, aggressiveness, baldness, blood hormones and average height, among other traits.

Thus we can say not only that all humanity springs from a common stock, but also that this origin is so recent that we are essentially of one race. The differences we tend to focus on are of the most superficial kind. The variability we see between individuals is actually beneficial for society because it increases the range of societal adaptability to environmental conditions. Finally, we may note that Africa is our universal homeland and the original garden of Eden. Thus when Bahá'u'lláh says that 'the earth is but one country and mankind its citizens', He is speaking factually, not metaphorically.

If race is really an invalid concept biologically, then it exists solely in the eyes of society. When I present this material as a public talk, I illustrate the arbitrariness of the grouping of people based on physical traits with a group of volunteers. I have about a dozen people come to the front of the auditorium. I say that since skin colour is clearly not a meaningful criterion for dividing people up, I will show them some other ways. I ask for volunteers who love hot weather to go to the left and those who love cold weather to go to the right. I say that here we have the heat-loving race on the left and the cold-loving race on the right, and the shopping mall-air-conditioned race in the middle. Then I say that I will show them the two different races that really do exist, and move the people around until I have men on one side and women on the other. I point out that these two groups differ in average height, weight, muscle mass, facial hair, baldness, life span, aggressiveness, bone density, skull thickness, blood clotting factor, sensitivity to pain, suicide rate, depression rate, alcoholism rate, hobbies, talkativeness, etc. Any two individuals from one 'race' (i.e. sex) are on average more like each other in these traits, irrespective of skin colour, than are two individuals of the same skin colour but different sex. And what do we do? We pick someone from this entirely different 'race' to be our partner in marriage! All over the world, people cross this very real gulf and share a bed and a house with someone so different that they often wonder if their spouse came from another planet. And yet, without this variety, the world would be a very dull place. But discrimination and suspicion between races is not just about skin colour; it is about other aspects of our social and psychological makeup. I discuss these next.

Race and Culture

There is a strong tendency to equate race with culture, as though culture were inherited in the genes. Thus blacks whose ancestors arrived in the United States two hundred years ago are asserted to be Afro-American in their cultural heritage. The demarcation is drawn very sharply based on skin colour and consists of very definite social expectations. Blacks are expected to like gospel/rap/jazz, but not classical or country or polkas. Why is this? Is this music trait inborn, as old-fashioned racial theories held? Of course not. No one is born with a feeling for any type of music or food or clothes, but acquires them by experience and by identifying with a group. There is no nationality gene, no language gene, no cultural gene, by which a newborn is automatically African or German or French. Culture consists of the habits, beliefs, language and customs common to a region. Some of the strongest identifiers of culture are diet, religion, holidays and recreation. By these measures US blacks are overwhelmingly American in culture. They are largely Christian, are major fans of football, watch fireworks on the Fourth of July and eat a largely American diet (with most of the 'ethnic' black food actually being related to a poor rural southern American rather than an African background). By comparison, in central Africa the population is largely Muslim or follows a tribal religion, has completely different holidays from Americans, eats different food, lives under a different governmental system and has different recreations. Parts of this region sanction the possession of multiple wives. American blacks and whites share a common culture that differs drastically from that of Africa, which itself is very diverse culturally. It is noteworthy that unity of race in Africa has not prevented prejudice or tribal warfare or oppression of minorities there any more than it has in Europe.

The problematic nature of identifying culture and race as synonymous becomes clearer when we examine multicultural/racial marriages. If someone has one Irish and one black parent, would we expect to see him in the St Patrick's Day parade? If someone has one black and one Japanese parent, what kind of music will she prefer? Why should not a French-Chinese child identify himself as French? Why should not a black woman enjoy Mozart, golf, French food and obscure foreign films with subtitles? We do, in fact, have white rap artists, an American Sumo wrestling champ and a black country music star (Charlie Pride).

The idea that one's race is a real entity, and that one's culture is determined by race, can be seen even more clearly to be false by examining another context. To an outsider, Japan is racially and culturally homogeneous. Yet there is a minority group in Japan which is discriminated against, but not because its members are foreigners or look different. This group in the feudal system was the caste that handled and buried the dead. As such, it was considered unclean. Most of the caste no longer perform this function but they are still discriminated against. Because it is not possible to identify them by appearance, genealogical registers are kept to identify these people by their ancestry. Thus we have a case where a group is racially and culturally identical to the majority but is still singled out for bad treatment. Another interesting case concerns majority Japanese who go to work overseas. If they are away for more than a few years, they find that upon their return they are shunned as 'outsiders' because they have been contaminated by the foreign culture.

There is nothing inherently wrong with identifying with a culture, nation or race to a limited degree.

The problem comes when boundaries between groups are assumed to be 'natural' and are made inviolate. Such boundaries are enforced by proscribing intermarriage, by limiting contact (with separate churches, for example) and by social pressure against individuals who make inappropriate choices in food, clothing or music. Groups with strong cohesion usually have disparaging terms reserved for outsiders. Such actions, while maintaining group cohesion, generate and perpetuate prejudice and division. Prejudice is not strictly a power relationship, but is about avoiding and disliking another based on group identity. Members of different disadvantaged minorities can all hate each other, and often do, even though in theory they share the same discrimination and should be in solidarity. Thus sharp demarcations between cultural groups are inseparable from prejudicial practices.

What I hope to have shown in this section is that attempts to draw a line around a group based on skin colour and identify that group as culturally homogeneous and distinct is both fallacious and pernicious. Enforcing group identity and uniqueness in fact is a cause of prejudice. Culture is not inherited, nor is some magic 'essence' of blackness (or Frenchness). Prejudice is not necessarily always about skin colour, but runs deeper than this, as I will discuss further in the next section.

The Biology of Racism

A curious feature of this problem of race is that there is a problem at all. Why should there be a tendency to discriminate between groups? Does this have any biological significance? After all, herds of cattle do not seem to segregate by colour markings; why do people? Clearly all species must be able to distinguish their own kind from others. The formation of groups for avoiding predators and the recognition of the proper individuals for mating would be impossible otherwise. But the tendency of humans to form strict barriers between self-group and 'other' can not be explained by species self-recognition tendencies. Even groups that look identical may avoid each other for reasons of religious or political affiliation.

A clue to this behaviour comes from looking at the social context of human evolution compared to other species. Some species are quite solitary, only coming together to reproduce. Humans, however, are incapable of surviving as solitary individuals. Other species, such as the American bison or African wildebeest, are usually found in herds of tens of thousands. In such species, no coherent groups are formed, only shapeless masses. Some species live in intermediate-sized groups of tens to hundreds. Most of the great apes, many monkeys, elephants, and some other species have this type of social structure. In the course of human evolution, it is likely that most of our ancestors lived in such groups. These groups are larger than one family unit, so the bond holding them together is not merely kinship, and yet the individuals in these groups must stay together in order to protect their young and themselves in times of danger.

This raises an interesting dilemma. Whereas the

basis for cohesion in the family group (a male horse and his harem, or a pride of lions) is largely based on kinship (an obvious basis for loyalty), and that in herding animals is purely species herd-based (bison are happy to be with any old group of other bison), what is the basis for cohesion in a group that is larger than the family but smaller than the herd? Studies of chimpanzees and baboons suggest that it is a combination of a network of personal relationships and a strong aversion to outsiders – animal xenophobia. For example, an individual attempting to join a particular group may need to hang around its fringes for a long time before becoming accepted. The tendency for individuals to avoid those who differ markedly in appearance from the average may be heritable[6] and may contribute to the sense of group identity.

It is only recently that people began living in communities larger than a hundred or so. During most of our time on this planet we have lived in small groups in which everyone looked the same, dressed the same, spoke the same and had some ancestors in common. The stranger or other group was usually a source of danger. The rituals, customs, dress and diet that defined the group represented the safety of membership, while looking or acting differently represented danger. I thus believe there is a strong drive deep in human nature to belong, to be part of a group. Our very survival has depended on loyal group membership for at least a million years. It is not very likely that the drive to belong is manifested as a specific inherited cue that identifies the group one belongs to, but rather is based on a general

sensitivity to things that are common to the group
one grows up in and a general aversion to things that
differ from this. Such a sensitivity allows individuals
to attach extreme emotional significance to various
symbols of group membership such as flags, totems,
clothing styles, speech, holidays, music and foods.
Such attachments can be very strong and lifelong.
This tendency to form groups has the unfortunate
consequence that race is an obvious trait for group
identification. A very dark person is obviously different in appearance from a very light person, and
strong group demarcations thus tend to result.

This same tendency to identify with a group also
suggests factors that may help break down these
racial barriers. The first factor is that what one sees
as 'strange' or different depends on what one has
been exposed to. Exposure as a child to a variety of
races and cultures in a positive friendly atmosphere
such as found at Bahá'í meetings can help prevent
the sense of 'us' versus 'them' from becoming too
fixed and rigid. Bahá'í administrative units are based
on municipal boundaries such that all Bahá'ís in a
town or area are of necessity part of the same
community. Creating separate 'churches' within a
town based on race, or any other criterion, is forbidden within a Bahá'í community and thus cultural
diversity and inter-race contact are maintained at all
times. The second factor is that strong emotional
attachment to a group or ideal not defined in terms
of race can help revise the 'us' and 'them' boundaries. Again, the Bahá'í teachings create a broader
loyalty. It is far from true that Bahá'ís are automatically lacking in prejudice. Rather, new Bahá'ís

enter the Faith with their existing baggage of biases but gradually unload them as they embrace the broader loyalties and universal symbols given to us by Bahá'u'lláh. Thus, the cure for racism is far from the legalistic emphasis on quotas, reparations and confrontation, and depends rather on familiarity and higher loyalty to overcome the natural human tendency we all have to identify those who look the same as 'us' and those who look different as 'them'.

A further human tendency that contributes to group xenophobia is for leaders to enhance their power by promising protection from an external threat. We witness the actual benefit of strong leaders when a primate troop is challenged by another group or by a predator. The dominant males typically lead the defence or decide when to retreat. In human society, also, strong leadership is necessary when a group is under attack. Unfortunately, it is also common for those seeking power to manufacture enemies or threats and to sharpen artificially the distinctions between groups, thus creating a 'problem' which they promise to resolve. American Senator Joseph McCarthy, who lead a vigorous campaign against alleged Communists in the 1950s, is an obvious example. If enough fear can be generated, then the followers of such power-seekers will become more loyal and dependent on them for protection. This is why radical political groups often try to provoke authorities to violence, so that the perception of physical threat will be added to the abstract hatred that binds the group together. When political power or personal influence is based on exclusivity and the sharpening of distinctions between groups, there is no incentive for leaders to build bridges and reduce intergroup antagonisms. To do so lessens the need people feel for strong leaders to protect them and thus undermines the leaders' power bases.

Merely to deplore this situation is of little consequence because leaders will naturally follow their own self-interest. What is helpful, however, is a different type of social structure that does not depend on exclusivity. A model for such a system is provided by the Bahá'í administrative order. In local Bahá'í communities the governing body consists of nine men and women elected at large. Because there is no campaigning for office, there is no opportunity for the people seeking leadership to make speeches that generate fear or create artificial needs. In fact, people who have a need for power are specifically discouraged by this system. If elected, they find themselves on a Local Spiritual Assembly that is governed by consultation and consensus and in which the constituent individuals have absolutely no authority outside of the Assembly itself. The Assembly's authority does not derive from the perception of threat by the members of the community but is innate. The person who is elected or appointed to a committee finds an arena for service but very little opportunity for personal glory. The reward structure of the Bahá'í administrative order favours those whose interest is in service and inclusivity and discourages those whose tendency is to create 'us' versus 'them' distinctions and confrontations.

The Ecology of Cultural Advance

The issue of race assumes the importance that it does because some races have such an economic advantage. There is presently intense rivalry between the US and Japan, for example, but the Japanese have earned respect by their economic power and are not looked upon as inferior by Americans. Since economic privilege tends to be held tightly once acquired, and because these economic disparities tend to support prevailing prejudices, it is worth examining the origins of these trends.

As European nations began to expand their spheres of influence in the 1400s, they found that sub-Saharan Africa and the continents of the Americas were easily conquered. The natural tendency to think that one's own group is superior was reinforced over and over during the succeeding centuries by these many conquests. It became natural to assume, and in fact became dogma, that the American Indians and black Africans were inherently primitive and inferior. If the backwardness of these regions is in reality not proof of their inferiority, then some other explanation of the rates of cultural advance in different regions of the world is needed.

I would like to bring an ecological perspective to bear on this problem. Whereas we are constrained very little by the natural environment at present, this was far from true during the course of the development of early human civilizations. The development of civilizations has been constrained by and guided by the geography and ecological context in which they originated. Examination of this ecological context throws considerable light on the rates of cultural progress in different regions of the world. In speaking of cultural progress, I am focusing on technological and social competencies such as agricultural productivity, the complexity and functionality of governmental units, the substitution of animal or machine power for human labour, etc. I do so not because such progress is the only kind – indeed it may take us away from human values – but because the wealth and power of a nation rest on this foundation, and it is the disparities in such technologically based wealth that have led to the differences in political power that have shaped our world. I am not judging what kind of culture is 'good' but rather what has determined the historical winners and losers of power struggles.

Whereas some degree of cultural development is possible based on hunting and gathering, advanced culture requires an agricultural basis. The earliest development of cities in all regions of the world coincides with the domestication of plants and animals. Domestication is a slow and difficult process, however, and most plants are not suitable for domestication. Early farmers gradually developed better crops by trial and error. The wheat plants that lost their seeds too easily were not harvested and saved for the next year's planting. Those too difficult to thresh were discarded. Those with bigger seeds were favoured. Only after thousands of years of such selection did the crops we now depend on develop suitable properties and a high enough yield that large numbers of people could be freed from farming to form artisan, merchant and soldier classes.

In the Middle East early farmers had a great advantage because large fields of several wild grains occurred naturally. These grains, including wheat, rye and oats, were annuals, naturally held their seed long enough to be harvested and had seeds large enough to be edible. Such plants could be adapted to primitive farming practices with very little modification.

Just as with plants, not all animals are suitable for domestication. The ideal domestic animal is easily tamed and follows a leader (for which the human becomes a substitute).[7] Of solitary animals, only the cat and the ferret have ever been domesticated. American Bighorn sheep live in herds but exhibit no submissive behaviour towards a leader and have never been tamed. Animals living in megaherds (many thousands together) such as bison or wildebeest similarly have never been tamed because there is no leader in such herds. Antelope and deer, which flee upon disturbance rather than standing their ground in group defence, are too skittish to be managed.

The Middle East had tamable species in abundance, including sheep, goats and camels. These species were domesticated very early in human cultures. By 6000 BP (Before Present) the Middle Eastern civilizations had tamed the major livestock species and thus had two key resources upon which they could build. When we look at the New World, however, we see a very different picture. Corn is a highly modified crop compared to its wild progenitors. For thousands of years after its initial domestication it was only a minor component of Indian diets, which included squash, tomatoes and potatoes. The morphology of corn ears had to go through thousands of years of modification before it became high yielding enough to support cities. Even then, corn is much more labour intensive than other grains because the individual ears must be harvested, shucked, dried and scraped. Even so, Indian civilizations such as the Aztec and Inca reached high levels of culture based on corn, but they were limited by a second factor: a lack of domestic animals. The llama and alpaca were domesticated but could not carry heavy loads and never spread out from the Andes. No other native large animals in the Americas are suitable for domestication. The American Indians thus lacked a ready supply of milk, meat and hides and had no source of muscle power for ploughing and carrying goods and people. The entire fabric of the Indian civilizations – cities, pyramids and all – was built without animal power and without the wheel, which was used only for toys. This severe obstacle to progress, not any deficit in their abilities or an innate inferiority, explains the backward state of the Indians when Europeans arrived.

The case of Australia is even more dramatic. The native Australians were among the most primitive people in the world when Australia was colonized by Europeans. Is this because these people are inherently inferior to Europeans? No, the cause may be attributable to an almost total lack of native animals and plants suitable for domestication. Kangaroos cannot be domesticated. Early Australians had only the dog as a domestic animal. Isolation prevented crops and animals domesticated elsewhere from reaching Australia.

Consideration of Africa is particularly relevant to the situation in America today. Bias by Europeans against Africans is typically greatest. The fact that no great civilization has ever arisen south of the Sahara fuels the implicit sense of superiority Europeans feel with respect to Africans. In Africa early peoples had domesticated plants and animals. However, another barrier to the development of an advanced culture existed in Africa: trade barriers. Trade is crucial for cultural advance because very few localities have all the requisite raw materials. Trade also facilitates the spread of agriculture and technology, ideas and inventions, art and literature, from one cultural centre to the next, thus speeding up development. Large scale trade may also be said to be a hallmark of advanced economies.

Up through modern times the primary form of transport of goods was by water, but in this Africa is notably deficient. In contrast, the Middle East and Southern Europe are ideally suited to trade. The Mediterranean, Caspian, Black and Red Seas are all relatively calm compared to the Atlantic, an import-ant consideration for small, fragile ships. There are short distances to travel on these seas, numerous islands exist to act as stepping stones, many long navigable rivers flow into them and natural harbours are abundant. None of these favourable conditions exist in Africa. The part of Africa bordering the Mediterranean (which has been civilized for thou-sands of years) is cut off from the interior by the Sahara desert. Caravans crossing the Sahara could only carry high value items such as gold and swords. Bulk items such as manufactured goods or clothing could not be transported by this route. The southern tip of Africa is cut off by the Kalahari desert. The western coast has few islands, treacherous currents, no ports and is open to the full force of the Atlantic, being therefore unsuitable for small, primitive craft. Even European vessels of the mid-1400s were barely able to traverse these seas. Furthermore, much of this coastline is desert, which caused great difficulty for early sailors such as the Portuguese who could not easily provision their ships as they sailed along the coast. If the Portuguese had not been intent on finding a route to India, they might have given up on the exploration of this coast because there were no people to trade with along it and no resources to plunder. The southern tip of Africa is especially treacherous and stormy. Whereas many major river systems in Northern Africa, the Middle East and Europe, such as the Nile, Rhine, Tigris and Thames, are navigable by small craft for much of their length, most of the rivers of sub-Saharan Africa are frequently interrupted by cataracts and falls. Whereas an American Indian could travel by canoe on the Mississippi system (with only short portages) from the Gulf to Colorado or Ohio or Minnesota or into the entire Great Lakes system and its tributaries all the way to the Saint Lawrence – and in fact they traded over this entire system – such was not true in Africa. The central African rain forest has been another great barrier to trade. As a final impediment, parts of Africa were until this century uninhabitable to humans or their livestock because of diseases

such as sleeping sickness. Thus while isolated
kingdoms grew up in Africa, such as Timbuktu and
the kingdoms of Benin, their further development
into empires and the development of their technological bases were impeded by their geographic
circumstances.

The most serious impediment to the development
of advanced technological civilization in Africa south
of the Sahara, however, was the absence of a
tradition of literacy, a deficiency also caused by
geographic isolation. While completely aliterate
nations can build substantial kingdoms, as indeed
were found in Africa, the development of more
advanced culture capable of technical mastery of the
environment requires writing and a number system.
Without these tools it is not possible to build upon
past experience and keep records.

The invention of writing, however, is no trivial
task. The development via picture writing to a true
written language has in each instance taken thousands of years. Europeans did not invent written
language and an alphabet themselves but received it
via diffusion and conquest over a prolonged period
after its origin in the Near East. However, they
acquired it well over three thousand years ago. In
contrast, writing was only introduced into Africa by
Arab traders and conquerors after the rise of Islam,
and then mainly to the eastern coastal areas such
as Mozambique. The rest of sub-Saharan Africa
remained essentially or completely without writing
until European conquest.[8]

Writing is particularly important for the kind of
technological advantages that allowed the Europeans

to conquer easily: guns, cannons, ships, efficient administrative structures, medicines, maps, compasses, binoculars, etc. The Romans could administer their far-flung empire only because edicts and laws could be transmitted to distant armies and governors via writing. When Europeans first made contact with Africans in the late 1400s, their technology was only slightly superior, but as time passed the accumulation of technological knowledge made possible by writing led to an overwhelming advantage that culminated in the complete conquest of Africa. Interestingly, the key development that allowed this conquest was medical advances which reduced the terrible toll disease took on European troops in Africa.

In addition to technology, cultural advance depends on the soft components of culture: religion, social institutions, family structure and concepts of time and of history. The environments of the different regions of the world have had a tremendous impact on these aspects of culture. Many of the earliest civilizations – the Egyptian, Mesopotamian and Chinese, for example – centred on rivers with broad flood plains where large-scale irrigation was possible. The necessity for control of the irrigation systems led to the development of strong and rigidly hierarchical governmental systems. These large governmental systems required accurate record keeping to predict flood seasons and to inventory grains stored in warehouses. They conducted large engineering projects, thus promoting the more rapid development of writing, numbers, arithmetic and geometry. Such river systems with predictable flooding of large level flood plains are lacking in sub-Saharan Africa.

As another example, the strong emphasis placed on the group in Oriental culture can in part be traced to the cultivation of rice as the dominant crop for thousands of years. Rice cultivation requires a great deal of cooperation between a group of farmers for maintenance of the irrigation systems and for planting the rice. A solitary farmer is at a distinct disadvantage. Emphasis on conformance to group norms and obedience to group decisions follows from these factors.

The fact of cold winters in Europe led to many cultural advances that proved advantageous. Because all food and fuel for the winter had to be secured ahead of time, extreme time-consciousness developed. The preoccupation with time led to a fascination with clocks in the early phases of the Industrial Revolution, which provided a spur to precision tool making and machining.[9] The large amount of time spent indoors during cold weather encouraged intellectual pursuits. The short growing season was also a spur to the invention and use of mechanical labour-saving devices in agriculture.

We must not ignore the major role that religion has had in shaping civilization. The Bahá'í view is that its role is central: that the revelations brought by the prophets have as their animating purpose the education of humanity and the advancement of civilization. In all the early major civilizations, large temple complexes formed the centre of the social order. Religion helped unify peoples into nations, providing a common outlook and holy days celebrated *en masse*. As religion progressed, more advanced concepts were introduced which enabled more civilized societies to develop. This stage of religion, however, required writing. Only very simple religious concepts can be transmitted in the form of myths and stories carried in an oral tradition. As noted above, however, a written language presupposes many other advantages of geography and climate such that a society capable of sustaining an educated class can exist. Thus technology and religion complement and feed back upon each other in the generation of more advanced civilization. In Africa south of the Sahara, no society ever reached the point of supporting writing, for the reasons mentioned above, and thus the beneficial effects of revealed religion were not felt until imported by Muslims and Europeans. Conversely, in Europe during the Dark Ages, religion kept literacy alive via the monks in their monasteries, so that it was a part of the culture when the society began to recover in the Renaissance and needed it. This speeded up the rate of technological advance of European society.

It is thus clear that geography and ecology have had major impacts on the development of civilization. Not all parts of the world were dealt the same hand. It is no accident that the Middle East was the earliest seat of civilization and has seen more great empires than any other region. Appropriate plants and animals for domestication were readily available, leading to the establishment of towns thousands of years earlier than elsewhere. Trade by land and sea was easy. The great inventions of many regions (the saddle, the chariot, writing) quickly passed through there and were adopted. None of these driving forces is a reflection on the native abilities of the peoples in these regions. Rather, some groups were lucky and some were not. With modern technology and trade it is possible to create a more level playing field for all regions of the world and for all the various peoples and races. In the interest of international stability, the nations of the world are being forced in this direction. The Bahá'í teachings urge that this equality is a moral obligation.

Spiritual Approaches

In the previous sections the biology and ecology of race and racism have been explored. This new perspective, it is hoped, cleared up various misconceptions about what race is, clarified the relationship between race and culture, and uncovered the roots of prejudice. But there are also roots of prejudice which are spiritual in nature and which no political or sociological analyses will uncover. Without this spiritual dimension, any analysis of racism is limited in depth and any solution offered is constrained in its effectiveness.

There are spiritual consequences to racism, consequences of which we must remain aware:

The theories and policies, so unsound, so pernicious, which deify the state and exalt the nation above mankind, which seek to subordinate the sister races of the world to one single race, which discriminate between the black and the white, and which tolerate the dominance of one privileged class over all others

– these are the dark, the false, and crooked doctrines for which any man or people who believes in them, or acts upon them, must sooner or later, incur the wrath and chastisement of God.[10]

It is clear, however, that the evil of racism cannot be eliminated by legalistic means. Once the most overt racist practices such as segregated schools and restaurants are eliminated by legal decrees, the remaining barriers are subtle and not easily legislated away. True equality is not merely a matter of legal status but rather involves spiritual qualities. Neither hiring quotas nor the politics of victimization achieve true equality and unity and in fact tend to take us further from them. Particularly pernicious is the new doctrine that racism is purely a power relation, such that only oppressors can be racist (or sexist or culturist). By this definition minorities cannot be racist. However, racism is not merely a matter of who has the wealth, but rather involves animosity and biases. Hatred is hatred, whatever excuse we use to justify it, and its presence precludes true equality because equality is based on reciprocity of trust and a sense of shared goals. What is needed is something that bridges the chasm separating hearts.

The first step in reaching the goal is remembering that no one is better than another in the sight of God. Outward attributes such as wealth are of no concern to God:

Know ye not why We created you all from the same dust? That no one should exalt himself over the other. Ponder at all times in your hearts how ye were created. Since We have created you all from one same substance it is incumbent on you to be even as one soul, to walk with the same feet, eat with the same mouth and dwell in the same land, that from your inmost being, by your deeds and actions, the signs of oneness and the essence of detachment may be made manifest. Such is My counsel to you, O concourse of light! Heed ye this counsel that ye may obtain the fruit of holiness from the tree of wondrous glory.[11]

The desire to exalt oneself above others is a very deep root cause of all kinds of prejudice. People want to be at the top of the heap, with the most money or biggest house or prettiest face. Such desires stem from an emptiness inside that people try to fill with status in place of real spiritual contentment. Thus prejudice against the overweight, the short and the ugly[12] arises in a very real sense from the same motivation that inspires racial prejudice: a desire to be superior. Even in a uniform social setting such as a suburban high school, groups form such as the jocks, eggheads and theatre types who look down on each other as being dumb, wimpy and strange, respectively. The PC (politically correct) movement in colleges, which is attempting to enforce language codes that prohibit any type of hate language, is a recognition that all these types of prejudice are from the same root; but because the PC movement does not recognize a spiritual solution, it has tried a legalistic one that is bound to fail. Only a change of heart will eliminate these types of offensive speech and action, but a change of heart requires a religious commitment. The first step in this religious commitment is the recognition of a God who created us from dust and in whose sight we are all judged on our inner, not our outer, qualities. In God's realm, the realm of spirit, none of us is fat or thin, rich or poor, handsome or ugly, but rather is generous or selfish, loving or hateful. Our soul does not have a skin colour nor does it have kinky or straight hair.

> God maketh no distinction between the white and the black. If the hearts are pure both are acceptable unto Him . . . God did not make these divisions, these divisions have had their origin in man himself. Therefore, as they are against the plan and purpose of God they are false and imaginary . . . It mattereth not what the exterior may be if the heart is pure and white within.[13]

Thus when we remember to look at people with a spiritual eye, outer qualities are no more important than the colour of a shirt, which can be changed in the blink of an eye. When my daughter was in kindergarten, she honestly could not remember which of her classmates was black or white; rather she noticed which ones were kind and which were mean. What a different world this would be if we all had such eyes!

The next step requires us to go beyond colour-blindness or lack of hatred and to achieve true unity. The Bahá'í view of unity is not one of uniformity, but rather one of harmony in diversity. That is, the vision is of a world of diverse peoples living harmoniously together, creating a colourful tapestry of lifestyles and cultures. Achieving this unity, however, requires a much deeper concept of unity than mere tolerance.

What is real unity? When we observe the human world we find various collective expressions of unity therein. For instance, man is distinguished from the animal by his degree or kingdom. This comprehensive distinction includes all the posterity of Adam and constitutes one great household or human family which may be considered the fundamental or physical unity of mankind. Furthermore, a distinction exists between various groups of humankind according to lineage, each group forming a racial unity separate from the others. There is also the unity of tongue among those who use the same language as a means of communication; national unity where various peoples live under one form of government such as French, German, British, etc.; and political unity which conserves the civil rights of parties or factions of the same government. All these unities are imaginary and without real foundation, for no real result proceeds from them. The purpose of true unity is real and divine outcomes. From these limited unities mentioned only limited outcomes proceed whereas unlimited unity produces unlimited result. For instance, from the limited unity of race or nationality, the results at most are limited. It is like a family living alone and solitary; there are no unlimited or universal outcomes from it.

The unity which is productive of unlimited results is first a unity of mankind which recognizes that all are sheltered beneath the overshadowing glory of the All-Glorious; that all are servants of one God; for all breathe the same atmosphere, live upon the same earth, move beneath the same heavens, receive effulgence from the same sun and are under the protection of one God. This is the most great unity, and its results are lasting if humanity adheres to it; but mankind has hitherto violated it, adhering to sectarian or other limited unities such as racial, patriotic or unity of self-interests; therefore no great results have been forthcoming. Nevertheless it is certain that the radiance and favours of God are encompassing, minds have developed, perceptions have become acute, sciences and arts are widespread and capacity exists for the proclamation and promulgation of the real and ultimate unity of mankind which will bring forth marvellous results. It will reconcile all religions, make warring nations loving, cause hostile kings to become friendly and bring peace and happiness to the human world. It will cement together the Orient and Occident, remove forever the foundations of war and upraise the ensign of the Most Great Peace. These limited unities are therefore signs of that great unity which will make all the human family one by being productive of the attractions of conscience in mankind.

Another unity is the spiritual unity which emanates from the breaths of the Holy Spirit. This is greater than the unity of mankind. Human unity or solidarity may be likened to the body whereas unity from the breaths of the Holy Spirit is the spirit animating the body. This is the perfect unity. It creates such a condition in mankind that each one will make sacrifices for the other and the utmost desire will be to forfeit life and all that pertains to it on behalf of another's good. This is the unity which existed among the disciples of His Holiness Jesus Christ and bound together the prophets and holy souls of the past. It is the unity which through the influence of the divine spirit is permeating the Bahá'ís so that each offers his life for the other and strives with all sincerity to attain his good-pleasure. This is the unity which caused twenty thousand people in Iran to give their lives in love and devotion to it. It made the Báb the target of a thousand arrows and caused Bahá'u'lláh to suffer exile and imprisonment forty years. This unity is the very spirit of the body of the world. It is impossible for the body of the world to become quickened with life without its vivification.[14]

Conclusion

It has become evident that our current approaches to race are woefully inadequate to meet the serious challenge before us. Yet this is not a problem that will go away on its own. The Bahá'í Faith urges that science and religion go hand in hand. In this context of race we can begin to see why this must be so. It is inadequate to talk of racial harmony when the assumptions so many people have are based on incorrect facts, assumptions that tend to produce subtle prejudice even in well-meaning people. Correcting these assumptions requires a dispassionate scientific investigation of history, geography, ecology and human biology. Doing so clears away the mental cobwebs that have interfered with clear thinking on this issue for so long. But merely creating a clear perspective is not enough. A spiritual basis must be found for achieving these goals or the will to act will be lacking. The Bahá'í Faith provides this spiritual basis, guidance, vision and motivation. By combining these two perspectives we can perhaps achieve 20/20 vision on the issue of race for the first time in human history.

2

Spiritual Synergy for a New Ecology

Introduction

The current state of our society's understanding of the environment is comparable to that of medicine of 60 years ago when the effect of behaviours (e.g. smoking) and attitudes (e.g. stress) on health were not yet understood. We recognize (sometimes) that a particular environmental problem exists, but are often unable to distinguish symptoms from diseases, causes from effects. Just as we used to suppress fever but now realize that it is a key component of the body's defences, we used to suppress all fires but now realize that many ecosystems cannot function without them and that fire suppression often leads to catastrophic conflagrations when a fire does inevitably start. For many environmental problems, however, we have not yet arrived at a balanced understanding. For example, beaches that are steam-cleaned to remove oil may turn out later to be less healthy than those left alone because whereas oil kills many organisms, the steam kills them all. Chlorine added as tertiary treatment for municipal waste may be more harmful to fish than the bacteria we seek to remove.

Ecological changes are often mediated through

many steps and by complex and convoluted pathways. When studying ecology, it is almost never safe to assume that the obvious cause is in fact the dominant or controlling factor. In the northeastern United States, moose are absent where deer are present. One might assume that these two related species compete, but in fact deer harbour a parasite to which moose are very susceptible, thus their non-overlapping ranges. A common method for tracing these causative pathways is called systems analysis. This method seeks to identify all of the processes at work in a system, quantifies their magnitudes and traces the feedback loops that govern the system. When we apply this technique to environmental problems, we find that our causal pathways must include human society. This much is well-known by ecologists. However, often the analysis stops at the point where inputs from society to the environment are identified. The factors governing these inputs are left undefined. A recent innovation is the attempt to link models of economic systems to ecosystem models. This is certainly a step in the right direction. However, the link between society and the environment is not merely economic. Instead, the mutual pathways of cause and effect extend all the way to the human heart. Our ability to recognize environmental problems, to assess correctly their causes and to respond in a timely and effective manner is intimately tied up with our world views, our set of values, our sense of community, and our view of our place and role in history. We do not in fact react to environmental issues based on rationality and cost-benefit analysis, but rather out of deep emotional needs, prejudices and assumptions.

A central determinant of one's world view, one's goals and fears and desires, is the presence (or absence) of a set of religious convictions. Bahá'ís believe that this connection is particularly strong and centrally relevant in the case of our environmental problems. Many of the 'easy' environmental problems (e.g. sewage treatment) have been solved (more or less) because a technological fix was the appropriate approach. The environmental problems we now face are more deeply connected with social values and structures and have been resistant to change mediated by the passage of laws.

The recognition by some that 'values' are central to the resolution of environmental problems has led to an effort to change our values by urging us to 'think green' and develop an 'eco-ethic'. Admirable as these attempts are, they are not capable of causing the transformation in society they seek to achieve. More than just good eco-intentions are called for because many of our environmental problems can be traced to causes having nothing to do with overtly environmental policies. Furthermore, it is not possible to change one's values piecemeal like changing one's shirt. What is needed is a change in the human heart that restores a spiritual balance and proper connection with the natural world.

Spiritual Disharmonies

Connections with Nature

Although our historical sense of separateness from nature has been amplified in recent urban life, wherein one stays air conditioned and food comes in packages rather than from living animals or plants, we may trace the roots of this separateness to the basic world view of western civilization. The view of humankind as separately created, apart from this physical world, and destined to rule over the inferior world of nature, is a dominant theme in our culture. Many Christians have viewed the natural world as a punishment for our fall from grace in the Garden of Eden. This view tends to create an uncaring and even hostile attitude towards nature. The view of many eastern religions is similarly that the physical world is inherently a place of pain and suffering. If the physical world is in fact our punishment, our prison, then it is difficult not to resent it and attempt to flee it in favour of the ethereal or fantastic.

Withdrawal from the world has traditionally been seen as the path to true spiritual life. For the last two thousand years the emphasis on the ascetic withdrawn life as the most spiritual was common. Monks and nuns in their monasteries have been the standard symbols of piety. The physical world has been viewed as gross, decaying, corrupt, imperfect and a source of temptation. In order to reach for higher spiritual values, people have sought to escape from the temptations of the flesh. Even games and sports were frowned upon by the church as worldly and frivolous. If such a perspective seems silly to us today, it is not because we are wiser but because we have gone to the opposite extreme – we worship material goods, pleasures and success. The flight from the physical world in past times represented by monks, hermits and dervishes is to an extent under-standable in the context of their times. The average man was figuratively, and often literally, hitched to the plough from sunrise until sunset. He could not read, had no books and had no time for contem-plation. The demands of a hard, dirty and toilsome existence precluded any deeper pursuit of the spiritual life. The ascetic monk, by foregoing family responsi-bilities and by being supported by the church, found the time for contemplation that the average person lacked. For centuries the only places with books and those who could read them were the monasteries.

The consequences of this attitude have seriously harmed our relations with nature. How is it possible to care about and be good stewards of a natural world that we see as dirty, decaying, imperfect and corrupt? Those who view sex as disgusting can hardly be very enamoured of a natural world in which sex is everywhere and central to the goings-on of the creatures. Indeed, historically people have not appreciated nature but have tried to conquer it, push it back and destroy it. Wildness was a thing to be eliminated in favour of the orderliness of farms and fields. Remnants of this attitude remain even today. Many modern affronts to nature are not due to mere carelessness or accident but to active voluntary destruction.

Restoring connectedness is thus key to the develop-ment of attitudes conducive to proper conservation and stewardship. The teachings of Bahá'u'lláh provide a framework for overcoming our separateness. Bahá'ís believe that humanity was not created separately from nature but evolved biologically as part of God's

plan.[1] We are thus inherently connected to the earth
and its life. The Adam and Eve story is understood
to be metaphorical.[2] Bahá'ís do not see nature as
corrupt, for it contained and gave birth to us.
Furthermore, the holy ground where man was born
is not a mythical garden but the very ground we walk
on. We are in the Garden and we should give it the
reverence it deserves. Realizing our origins and our
connection to nature, we should not hold it in
contempt but in awe. The things of this world
are natural to this world and not reprehensible.
Bahá'u'lláh states that the things of this world, such
as food, clothing, arts and fine objects, are not
forbidden to us as long as they do not come between
us and God. He praises those who are steadfast in
poverty and adversity but also those who use their
wealth to aid God's cause. The current low status
our society gives to the working person and the
high status given to the idle rich are reversed by
Bahá'u'lláh; work performed in the spirit of service
to all humankind is stated to be a form of worship.
This reconnects the daily life of the ordinary person
with his or her higher spiritual self. It reminds him
that every job should contribute to the greater good
and should be an arena for pride, ethics, quality,
craftsmanship and service. With this goal in mind, an
exploitative attitude towards nature becomes less
possible because the horizon of each worker is
broadened beyond the pay cheque he or she receives.

Bahá'u'lláh urged the monks to abandon their
monasteries and to do work useful to society. He
further urged them to marry. Marriage is raised in
status by Bahá'u'lláh. The family, not the isolated

individual, is the basic spiritual unit in the Bahá'í Faith, and the reproductive drive expressed within its bounds is sanctified. Purity is still enjoined but it means fidelity to one's spouse, not sexual abstinence. Thus the need to deny physical urges to avoid damnation is abolished, along with the overall contempt for nature as merely a source of temptation and of punishment for original sin. If our bodies are not corrupt and disgusting, then perhaps that stigma can be removed from the rest of nature as well.

Reverence

Western peoples have very little respect for nature *per se*. We love to holiday at a beautiful place, but only because it is pleasurable. Nature is merely another consumable item of our endlessly consuming society. When we examine primitive cultures, in contrast, we see a distinct reverence for nature based on a feeling of kinship with nature spirits. That is, they have reverence for the wind because it is a spirit like theirs, though more powerful and majestic. In this context the animals are literally our brothers and are thus worthy of respect.

Attempts to restore reverence by reviving primitive religion are doomed to failure, however, because we no longer really believe that there is a spirit of the wind and a spirit of the waters. Saying that 'the Earth is our Mother', for example, is inconsistent with a belief that life on earth is sinful and is our punishment for Eve's transgression. We cannot retreat but must move onward to the wisdom given us by the modern prophets.

Bahá'u'lláh leads us to understand that nature does not equal God, nor is God in the trees and rocks; rather nature is a manifestation of the names and attributes of God:

Say: Nature in its essence is the embodiment of My Name, the Maker, the Creator. Its manifestations are diversified by varying causes, and in this diversity there are signs for men of discernment. Nature is God's Will and is its expression in and through the contingent world. It is a dispensation of Providence ordained by the Ordainer, the All-Wise.[3]

The Bahá'í writings describe two 'books' of God: nature (illumined by science) and divine revelation. Both are necessary for spiritual advancement, which is why the Bahá'í teachings emphasize the harmony of science and religion. The book of nature opens up many spiritual vistas when perceived with the eye of detachment and submission:

. . . whatever I behold I readily discover that it maketh Thee known unto me, and it remindeth me of Thy signs, and of Thy tokens, and of Thy testimonies. By Thy glory! Every time I lift up mine eyes unto Thy heaven, I call to mind Thy highness and Thy loftiness, and Thine incomparable glory and greatness; and every time I turn my gaze to Thine earth, I am made to recognize the evidences of Thy power and the tokens of Thy bounty. And when I behold the sea, I find that it speaketh to me of Thy majesty, and of the potency of Thy might, and of Thy sovereignty and Thy grandeur. And at whatever time

I contemplate the mountains, I am led to discover the ensigns of Thy victory and the standards of Thine omnipotence.[4]

Not only does the world of nature give us indications of God's attributes, it also teaches specific spiritual lessons to those who would learn:

Every man of discernment, while walking upon the earth, feeleth indeed abashed, inasmuch as he is fully aware that the thing which is the source of his prosperity, his wealth, his might, his exaltation, his advancement and power is, as ordained by God, the very earth which is trodden beneath the feet of all men. There can be no doubt that whoever is cognizant of this truth, is cleansed and sanctified from all pride, arrogance, and vainglory.[5]

Furthermore, the imagery of nature is a key vehicle for communicating spiritual truths. This has perhaps never been so evident as in the writings of Bahá'u'lláh which are full of metaphors and images taken from nature. Such images bypass the intellect and go straight to the heart, enabling profound truths to be communicated even to those devoid of formal education and carrying us to places that logic alone cannot.

The above passages make it clear that without a connection to nature a fully urban, man-made world becomes spiritually impoverished. Without nature we are bereft of a spiritual tongue, are left devoid of visions of grandeur and majesty, and remain unschooled in the lessons of humility. This is why nature deserves our reverence: our very spiritual growth depends upon its integrity and wholeness. The restoration of reverence is a key step along the path to a healed human psyche.

A Short-Term Perspective

One of the most serious contributors to environmental destruction is the extreme short-sightedness of society's responses to its problems. This is particularly the case for environmental problems because many of them are cumulative over decades. It is often far easier to prevent such environmental problems as soil loss than it is to fix them. In addition, solutions to these problems may take decades to develop. For example, it was known at least 20 years ago that the potential existed for high altitude ozone to be destroyed by man-made compounds such as refrigerants. Only grudgingly was a small amount of research funding made available to document the problem and study high altitude atmospheric chemistry. More seriously, little effort was put into developing alternative refrigerants. One of the few companies to work on this problem was DuPont, which has spent a great deal of money over at least ten years developing new compounds. The potential seriousness of ozone depletion is now established and makes us realize that the solution to this problem should not have depended on whether some company was willing to invest its own money in solving it. Without DuPont's far-sightedness the ozone hole problem would be even more serious than it already is. Other examples of such short-sighted behaviours include research on solar power, protection of coastal fisheries and protection of groundwater quality.

What accounts for such short-sightedness? I would argue that it is not an inherent characteristic of large organizations, since long-term planning is often in evidence: the development of our interstate highway system, development of integated international tele-communications systems, rural electrification in the 1940s and regional flood control projects are examples. When we observe that such efforts are possible, the failure to plan ahead and work together in other areas stands out even more sharply. Three strong forces contribute to short-sightedness in our culture today: materialism, apocalyptic views of the future and what we may call religious me-ism.

As religious convictions have declined in this century (as evidenced by increased secularization of religious holidays and declining obedience to religious teachings against cohabitation and having children out of wedlock) materialistic attitudes have increased. This is no accident. Without the bond of community created by religion and the spirit of service arising from it, people are left increasingly empty and without any higher purpose than their own needs and desires. Such a motivational base is inherently selfish and short-term. Few feel constrained by the requirements and long-term needs of the society in which they are living. In addition, the consequent general feeling of isolation and non-involvement so many feel removes the incentive for any self-sacrificial contribution towards long-term or broader social goals.

Effectively combating loss of faith, the isolation of

the individual, and the dissolution of social bonds that lead to excessive and corroding materialism cannot be accomplished by tent meeting revivals. The established religions have become so fragmented that they have lost much of their credibility. What is needed is a renewal of the essence of religion such that religion again becomes central to the moral and social life of society. Bahá'ís aver that their Faith is exactly this renewal, a Faith devoid of the superstitious encrustations that test the reason of educated people, absent of the conflict between science and religion that is a barrier to faith, and with a set of teachings appropriate to the modern world. When religion is reborn and resumes its rightful place in the hearts of individuals and the life of society, materialism retreats to its proper place as the servant of our spiritual goals, not the master. Equally important, Bahá'u'lláh shows us clearly that our spiritual fate as individuals is intimately tied up with that of society at large.

A type of short-sightedness that is particularly manifest in our dealings with the environment is engendered by fears of apocalypse. Literal reading of scripture has convinced many that when Christ returns the physical earth will be replaced by a new one created for His followers. This belief is so pervasive, even though not discussed much openly, that it is manifest throughout our culture. Influential intellectuals such as Tolstoy, Sartre and Marx were inspired by this image of the destruction of the old world to be followed by a glorious new world, and promulgated a secular version of apocalypse. Mass destruction followed by salvation for a chosen few is even a common theme in popular movies (for example, *Earthquake*, *Towering Inferno*, *The Poseidon Adventure*). Throughout the last two thousand years there have been recurrent waves of apocalyptic fervour. The 1830s and 1970s were decades when apocalyptic fervour was particularly strong. The consequence of these views for environmental issues is serious because it encourages a truncated view of the future. Predictions of apocalypse and rapture typically give 'soon', meaning the next few decades, as the time frame for the Lord's return. In this context one should still go about the business of business (i.e. making a living) in the short term but the longer term issues of protection of wildlife and loss of topsoil are past that truncated time horizon beyond which the world will be (we are told) incinerated and are thus not likely to be addressed.

History teaches us, however, that literal interpretation of scripture is fraught with peril, especially in the case of the Book of Revelation. Hardly a major historical event, solar eclipse or comet has been noted in the last several hundred years but someone has claimed that it heralds the final battle of Armageddon and the destruction of the world. Prophetic images, however, are nearly always metaphorical. The very reason that the Jews failed to follow Christ was that He failed to fulfil the prophecies literally, even though He fulfilled them inwardly. The purpose of metaphorical language is to separate the 'wheat' of humanity from the 'chaff', those with spiritual eyes from the 'blind'. The images of destruction accompanying the Lord's advent symbolize the overturning of institutions, of prejudices, of vested interests that His coming achieves. A discussion of these points may be found in *The Book of Certitude* by Bahá'u'lláh.

The Bahá'í view of apocalyptic events foretold in the Bible is that they do in fact pertain to that great Day when the Lord will come in the station of the Father, that this Day will be accompanied by great convulsions and turmoil, that this Day has already arrived with the coming of Bahá'u'lláh and that the prophecies concerning that Day are even now being fulfilled. The destruction foretold, however, will not be of the physical earth. The world will not end, nor mankind be destroyed, but the old world of ideas and institutions will be rolled up and a new one laid out in its stead.

The Bahá'í understanding of the prophecies of the establishment of God's Kingdom on earth has several consequences. First, since the world will continue into the future, our treatment of nature matters. Second, God's plan is for this world, hence we are living in God's House, not just our private sandbox. If we defile the air and water, strip away the forests and extinguish species, then we are opposing God's plan for the future of humankind. Consequently, good stewardship of nature becomes not just a matter of preserving parks for our pleasure or maintaining the quality of life for our children, but a sacred responsibility.

The Lord of all mankind hath fashioned this human realm to be a Garden of Eden, an earthly paradise. If, as it must, it findeth the way to harmony and peace, to love and mutual trust, it will become a true abode of bliss, a place of manifold blessings and unending delights. Therein shall be revealed the excellence of humankind, therein shall the rays of the Sun of Truth shine forth on every hand.[6]

The final source of short-sightedness is religious me-ism, that is, the misguided view that the sole purpose of religion is to save oneself and that one's responsibility is fulfilled once one becomes a believer. If one believes that the material world is irredeemable, is doomed to sin, and will be destroyed in the apocalypse, if you believe, in other words, that the devil won, then the only logical course is to save oneself like a rat abandoning a sinking ship. Bahá'u'lláh warns against those who profess faith in the hope of a reward, whether in this world or the next. One's faith should be based on 'He is God' and not on a fear of death. Belief based on fear is subject to being forgotten during times of good health, comfort and wealth, as indeed many have forgotten today. Emphasis on the preservation of the self via salvation makes the goal appear to be only belief, not action. The Bahá'í view is that belief can only truly be manifested through action.

O SON OF MY HANDMAID!
Guidance hath ever been given by words, and now it is given by deeds. Every one must show forth deeds that are pure and holy, for words are the property of all alike, whereas such deeds as these belong only to Our loved ones. Strive then with heart and soul to distinguish yourselves by your deeds. In this wise We counsel you in this holy and resplendent tablet.[7]

The emphasis on individual salvation has serious repercussions for the stewardship of nature. The belief that the world is inherently corrupt and decaying and only getting worse leads to a callousness towards our mistreatment of nature, because the resulting ugliness is only to be expected! Furthermore, if nature and society are seen as irredeemable, then the consequence is a turning away from them. This is exactly what has happened in certain circles, with a consequent apathy to environmental issues.

The Bahá'í teachings offer a completely different perspective on the perfectibility of humanity. First, the ever-advancing nature of society is unreservedly asserted. Second, the spiritual progress of the individual is understood to be intimately connected to the condition of society. Thus the individual and society both need to be reformed. This extends also to the natural world, whose beauty, or lack thereof, has a definite effect upon our spirits.

> We cannot segregate the human heart from the environment outside us and say that once one of these is reformed everything will be improved. Man is organic with the world. His inner life moulds the environment and is itself also deeply affected by it. The one acts upon the other and every abiding change in the life of man is the result of these mutual reactions.[8]

Third, the Bahá'í Faith emphasizes a life of service to others and not a religious life devoted solely to pious worship. It is only through service that the quality of our belief can be demonstrated and only by service that we can truly grow spiritually. The emphasis on service extends to the teaching in the Bahá'í writings that work performed in the spirit of service is a form of worship. That is, work performed in a spirit of service does not merely add 'good deeds' points to one's spiritual record but is actually equivalent to worship in a temple. This principle has the most profound consequences for our interactions with nature. Nature is fairly safe while everyone is in church. It is while performing our jobs that the real ecological devastation is done. While environmental protection laws have helped a great deal, much of the destruction and pollution we now face can only be solved by an awareness on the part of each person of his or her stewardship role. As mentioned earlier, this is unlikely to be satisfactorily achieved by exhortations to 'think green'. On the other hand, remembering that one's work is worship can have a profound effect. Before the gas station owner dumps waste oil in the vacant lot next door, he may pause to ask if this is truly being of service. The logging tractor operator may ask whether it is really respectful of God's Kingdom to drive his equipment back and forth through the stream. In this way environmental mindfulness becomes connected deeply with the human heart and with everyday life.

It should be noted that the Bahá'í Faith restores a historical perspective to our lives. In a time dominated by sound bites and stroboscopic music videos, the Bahá'í revelation brings the past alive, makes it a part of our personal histories, and connects it to the future and our destiny. Ultimately a personal sense of meaning is impossible outside of the context of the grand historical unfoldment of God's great plan. The stage for this grand plan is the world of nature, which alone is capable of nurturing and sustaining us.

I have argued here that a feeling of separateness, a lack of reverence, and short-sightedness are not natural conditions but are deficiencies arising from lack of true faith. These attitudes are at the root of our failure to address environmental problems adequately. More detail on these topics may be found in Dahl[9] and White.[10]

Practical Steps

It is the firm conviction of Bahá'ís that action can only truly succeed when it is based on spiritual principles. Otherwise, advocates of 'peace' may end up promoting the violent overthrow of governments and those trying to help the poor may actually worsen their plight. In environmental efforts, especially, it is easy to squander resources to little benefit.

The world-embracing vision of Bahá'u'lláh provides a context for ascertaining the root causes of environmental destruction and for looking beyond the superficial causes often studied by scientists. Bahá'u'lláh's writings reveal three rather surprising major causes of environmental destruction: war, prejudice and the disadvantaged status of women in the developing world. The linkages between these factors are particularly important to examine.

War and the Environment

War in the twentieth century has become a tremendous threat to the environment. War has the effect of shortening planning horizons and shifting resources to immediate survival needs. During World War Two in the US, for example, timber cutting increased in the national forests in the interest of defence while investments in long-term environmental benefits were reduced to a bare minimum. Our current needs for long-term and consistent investment in solar power, safer nuclear power, safer agricultural chemicals, wildlife preservation and alternatives to chloroflurocarbons (among others) are such that we dare not divert our attention from these efforts even for a moment.

The distracting and diverting effect of war is greatly exaggerated in the case of civil war, which is now the main type of conflict in the world. During a civil war, basic institutions such as forestry and agriculture ministries become disrupted or are unable to gain access to portions of the country. In the absence of game wardens, agriculture experts and forestry officers, depredations on the environment may become severe. Sanitary facilities may likewise quickly fall into disrepair. Guerilla troops, displaced populations or marching armies may devastate wildlife.

The direct effects of modern war are now far more odious and permanent than at any time in the past. For example, in Vietnam the United States used defoliation over hundreds of square miles to uncover enemy troops. Recovery of tropical forests cleared

Asian Orange

on this kind of scale is very slow. Tree establishment is limited by seed dispersal and only a few species have seeds which disperse more than half a mile. In addition, a large cleared area tends to become choked with weedy vegetation which greatly slows down tree establishment. The effect is much worse than logging because logging does not destroy all the thousands of seedlings present under the forest. In addition, after logging many species sprout from the stumps. Defoliation thus has consequences that may last for centuries. In the recent war in Kuwait, the artillery, carpet bombing and concentrated assault by tens of thousands of heavy vehicles had the effect of denuding large areas of any vegetation. Plants in desert environments typically are slow growing and long-lived. Conditions favouring plant establishment occur only rarely. These effects are of course exacerbated when large areas are so denuded that there is no seed source for plant establishment. Recovery may thus take decades or longer. Under the right conditions, such disturbances could cause dormant dune systems to become active again. Once dunes start to move they can generally only be stabilized by a much wetter climatic interval. Thus modern war has the capacity to wreak environmental havoc on a scale and permanence never before seen.

The concern of Bahá'ís with peace is both fundamental and central to their beliefs. It is not merely that Bahá'ís favour peace because it is a 'good thing'. Rather, it is the central and animating purpose of the revelation of Bahá'u'lláh to establish a united world at peace. All the religious books of the past proclaim that some day peace will reign. Bahá'ís believe, and

Bahá'u'lláh proclaims, that these promises are all fulfilled in this day and in His person; that is, this is the day foretold by all the prophets of old, when the lion shall lie down with the lamb and the swords shall be beaten into ploughshares. The means for achieving this goal are not merely pious hope, prayer and wishful thinking, but rather a specific set of world-embracing, visionary teachings that can transform both the individual and society. Two of the most central of these teachings which will bring about peace are the elimination of prejudice and the equality of men and women, which feature in the next two sections. Other teachings in this regard include collective security, the adoption of an international auxiliary language and increased fairness of the global economic system. None of these components of a true peace are merely political arrangements or treaties, but rather are spiritual in their nature.

Prejudice

At first glance it may not seem obvious that prejudice could affect the environment. One connection lies in the consequences of prejudice in a developing country. Much of the environmental destruction in these countries results from slash and burn agriculture, tree cutting for fuel, farming of hillsides, and poaching. Such activities are typically carried out by the poorest segments of society who generally are members of some minority or disenfranchised group. Such groups usually do not have access to education and thus are ill-equipped to carry out these activities in a way that protects the environment. For example, Haiti was ruled for several generations by a brutal dictatorship which effectively disenfranchised the majority of the population. Haiti is consequently 95% deforested and the people practise agriculture at a primitive and destructive level.

In addition to education, the other key ingredient of ecologically sound agriculture is capital. The disenfranchised are cut off from this resource as well. In developed countries a major source of the prosperity of farmers and the spread of effective farming techniques has been voluntary farmers' organizations such as marketing co-ops, the Grange, the 4-H and soil conservation districts. Those without education are again largely cut off from opportunities to organize themselves.

A further serious impact of prejudice on the environment results from group conflicts. Tribal hatreds and power struggles often lead to civil or guerilla war, with concomitant environmental destruction. Even when open war does not result, however, the sense of a unified society is destroyed. This leads to each group trying to grab as much for itself as it can. In this situation, any attempt to preserve wild habitat, for example, is seen by one group or the other as being at their particular expense and tends to be resisted. Intergroup conflict also tends to interfere with efforts that require overall cooperation for their achievement or which are on a long time-scale.

As is evident from the situation in the US today, laws may remove barriers to equality but they do not bring about racial amity. What is needed is a spiritual transformation of both the individual and society. This is the very transformation that Bahá'u'lláh's teachings aim to produce. Bahá'u'lláh has made it clear that world peace cannot be attained until unity is firmly established. He has also placed the elimination of prejudice at the top of His followers' spiritual agendas, because in this day it is no longer acceptable to praise God and condemn one's neighbour. Bahá'ís do not give the fight against prejudice mere lip service but are active in their struggle against it. The rights of minorities are protected in the Bahá'í administrative order. Bahá'í community boundaries are based on municipal boundaries, so that all Bahá'ís in a particular town meet together regardless of race; the separation of congregations on racial, ethnic, economic or other lines is forbidden. Bahá'í communities worldwide seek to be models of racial and ethnic harmony. The goal of all Bahá'í communities is preservation of ethnic diversity and culture in the context of harmonious and equal interaction.

Overall, then, we see that prejudice, by being a major cause of environmentally destructive wars, by preventing cooperation for the common long-term environmental good, and by creating disenfranchised groups that lack the educational and financial resources to make a living in an environmentally sound way, is indeed a major contributor to our global environmental problems. Laws will not cure this ill: Bahá'ís believe that only the healing message of Bahá'u'lláh can.

The Status of Women

The status of women as a disadvantaged section of humanity is a major, hidden cause of environmental degradation. One reason is that the number of people on earth is the ultimate determinant of the level of stress on ecosystems. As the population grows we produce more waste and require more farmland, we catch more fish and cut more trees. The impact of human populations on the natural environment is most severe in the developing countries, which is also where population growth is greatest. In some of these countries continued growth threatens to denude the land of all vegetation. Two things have been found clearly to decrease the population growth rate, even to zero: economic development and the education of women.[11] When women are given even minimal educational opportunities, they tend to reduce the number of children they have to the number they can raise well.

The importance of women in economic development, particularly in the underdeveloped nations, has generally not been appreciated. Development assistance has tended to focus on large projects such as dams and irrigation systems. But development is a process which involves the whole culture. In the typical third world village, women are generally accorded few rights, literacy is low, hygiene is poor, infant mortality is high, and economic activity is focused on subsistence farming. Even a small increase in the economic and educational level of the women in this village leads to a major drop in infant mortality because of easily implemented changes in infant nutrition and hygiene, such as boiling drinking water. Such a drop in infant mortality is usually followed by a drop in the birth rate because women feel more confident that some of their children will survive. This means that women can devote more time to the education and training of the children they already have, yielding a more competent generation to follow them. Even in developed countries children from large families tend to have lower test scores due to reduced contact with adults. The smaller number of children require less food which means that the adults can spend more time on development activities. Women spend less time pregnant (by as much as several years) and thus have extra energy for social and economic activities. In addition, the increase in hygiene that results from education of women (who do most of the cooking and cleaning) also leads to better village hygiene and reduced illness. Major portions of many third world village populations suffer from transient or chronic illness, parasites or poor nutrition at any given time. Reductions in this level of ill health due to improved hygiene can free up enormous energies for economic development.

Women are involved in many economic activities in villages, such as farming, sewing, making baskets and selling produce at the market. Even modest education can lead to more efficient business practices, increasing overall economic development.

The education of women also advances overall educational goals. Economic development depends on universal increases in education of all types – technical, general literacy, cultural. As the first educators of children, educated women can play a key role in preparing their children for intellectual success, thus raising a generation even more prepared to face an increasingly complex and sophisticated world.

Many programmes have been established for educating women, but progress has not been as great as hoped. This is because educating women is often seen in rural subsistence cultures as conflicting with the basic status of women as secondary and subservient to men. Thus men resist these changes. When women are given vocational training and succeed in gaining increased economic success from their small businesses, their husbands often take the profits and prevent any reinvestment in the growth of the business. Likewise, advertising the use of birth control does not have the desired effect if women have no control over the decision to have children and men feel their manhood threatened by it. Finally, under the severe economic constraints operating in third world countries, educating women often receives a very low priority even when not opposed directly, because its utility is not obvious.

Separately, economic development, birth control and the education of women each lowers the birth rate, but only to a small degree. It is when they are combined that large results are seen and that the synergy of development and women's education can be achieved. In the developed world these processes occurred over hundreds of years, but in the third world we cannot wait that long because of the scale of human suffering and environmental destruction already occurring. A complete, systemic, unified approach is needed to achieve these goals. Such an approach is provided by the Bahá'í teachings.

Whereas it is fashionable to try to make it appear that past religious traditions are compatible with equal rights for women, the explicit teachings in the Jewish, Christian, Muslim and Hindu scriptures all specify a subservient status for women. They must keep their faces or heads covered, remain silent, and are excluded from the religious hierarchy. Only the Bahá'í scriptures specifically state this principle of equality and in fact emphasize its importance. Bahá'ís understand this change in divine teachings in terms of social and religious evolution. In past ages life depended more on the strength and even the aggression of men, whereas now equality is more compatible with the demands of a technologically advanced society ruled by law.

The fact that the principle of equality of the sexes is part of a complete Bahá'í social system means that the impediments to the education of women should fade as a society adopts a Bahá'í way of life. Men's fear over loss of control is lessened because the Bahá'í way of life is based entirely on consultation rather than on raw power and authority. The importance of education generally and of women as the first educators of children in particular is emphasized repeatedly in the Bahá'í scriptures. These teachings are being put into practice daily and on an increasing scale in Bahá'í communities around the world. The gradual change that results can be illustrated by considering the story of one particular village in India where the entire village became Bahá'ís. At first, as was customary, the women could not attend

Bahá'í meetings but listened from outside the room. After becoming more familiar with the Bahá'í teachings, the women joined the men in the meetings and began to participate in the discussions and deliberations. In a short time they established literacy classes for adult women to help them catch up with the men. This example could be augmented with hundreds of others. With the barriers to education and participation in society removed, progress on environmental issues, economic development and population control is possible.

Conclusion: Spiritual Synergy

We have seen the potential for synergy when spiritual principles are applied simultaneously to multiple domains of human affairs, because all of the key social and environmental issues are multiply connected. Prejudice leads to war, which is destructive to the environment, and inhibits development that is necessary for solving environmental problems. Oppression of women is another form of prejudice. Equality of women and men is a key prerequisite for a lasting peace. It also reduces the population growth rate, which is both a cause of war and of over use of resources. It is obvious that these multiple connections of cause and effect, of attitude and social structure, cannot be changed piecemeal but require that a coherent system replace the current incoherent one. Such a coherent system, that harmonizes all the elements of individual and social life, is provided by Bahá'u'lláh.

3

Creativity

The Divine Gift

Introduction

The Bahá'í view of life and society is not one of static and rigid traditions, institutions and rituals but one of constant change. The generative, developmental impulse is given primacy. Ritual is minimized and the outward forms of religion are made flexible and adaptable. Emphasis is placed on inner spiritual development made manifest in service.

As a consequence of the emphasis on change and development in the Bahá'í Faith, its adherents must become good problem-solvers. A flexible, creative mental attitude is necessary. As members of Bahá'í consultative bodies such as Local Spiritual Assemblies, large numbers of Bahá'ís are actively engaged in problem-solving. Bahá'ís are also engaged in creating new institutions, new attitudes and new ways of behaving on a scale never before attempted. Almost every tradition, prejudice and institution of the past is called into question by the all-embracing teachings of Bahá'u'lláh. Bahá'ís have also begun to address practical problems such as social and economic development and the environment. Therefore the degree to which we, as builders of the New World Order, must be truly original in our thought is correspondingly great.

The purpose of this chapter, therefore, is to explore the nature of creativity and innovation and offer some thoughts on enhancing them. As a model for creativity I take not the arts, but science. The role of Bahá'í spiritual principles in the arts and of the arts in Bahá'í life has been admirably discussed previously.[1] However, the arts are primarily a means for emotional and intellectual expression rather than practical problem-solving. Furthermore, in the arts no objective criteria exist for judging success or truth. Thus if a rock star attributes his creativity to drugs, it is very difficult to evaluate this claim. While many would grant that religion has a role to play in the arts, most people view practical fields such as science, engineering and management as subject only to reason and economics. However, this view is directly responsible for many dislocations due to technology, dehumanized work places and the in-efficient use of human potential in many realms of endeavour. I contend that there is a direct and necessary link between creativity in applied fields and a spiritual approach to one's work. My model for studying this linkage is the practice of science. I have focused on science because the creative act in science must result in a practical, workable solution to some problem. There is an objective criterion for judging success in science by which we can evaluate whether a particular attitude or behaviour helps or hinders creativity. It is thus a potentially useful model for learning about the application of spiritual principles in the context of concrete problem-solving. I hope to show that the application of certain basic spiritual teachings of the Bahá'í Faith is conducive to increased creativity and enhanced problem-solving capacity in practical fields such as science and also in other contexts. Thus I propose a positive feedback loop of better and more creative problem-solving leading to a more successful development of Bahá'í institutions and to a spiritualization of the working life of individuals, which provides the foundation for even more successful and creative problem-solving.

The Creative Act

Not everything done in science may be considered creative. A major part of the edifice of science consists of a toolbox of techniques and instrumentation. We are interested here in the subset of scientific problem-solving which we may label truly creative. Such work is easily recognized in retrospect; virtually every scientist who makes it into the history books has done creative work (though not all his or her work would qualify). The historical perspective selects those who were both creative and correct. It is much more difficult to evaluate creative work as it is being produced. There are many characteristics shared between the truly creative and the misguided. Bold hypotheses, eloquent presentation and beautiful analogies characterize both groups. What separates the crank (such as those who continualiy invent perpetual motion machines) from the true innovator, in my opinion, is a fatal flaw in a key spiritual dimension of the creative process in the crank. Such flaws include a lack of humility, self-aggrandizement, lack of introspection and dishonesty. Please note that I am not suggesting that great scientists are model human beings or saints. In fact, they tend to avoid church-going and have little interest in participating in charitable organizations.[2] However, the focus caused by work that is reality-oriented and provides constant feedback leads to certain positive spiritual consequences. It is impossible, for example, to conduct research while hung over or in a rage. Most creative scientists are particularly conscious of the factors which interfere with their work. Likewise, because the creative act is subtle and easily disrupted, the connection between spiritual principles and concrete results is perhaps more easily demonstrated in the context of science where objective testing of results is possible.

Hubris and Humility

Making creative contributions in science requires a delicate balance between *hubris* and humility. *Hubris* is defined as insolence or arrogance resulting from excessive pride. It is generally a pejorative term, but in fact insolence and arrogance (of a special kind) are essential qualities for making truly innovative discoveries. The creative scientist is insolent, having little respect for authority, because his experience is that authority is often wrong. In fact, his career depends upon being able to show that the current wisdom is wrong or at least that it has overlooked something important. He is arrogant because he expects to be able to uncover the secrets of nature by his own power. This is *hubris* in the sense exhibited by Prometheus who stole fire from the gods, though it is often viewed by outsiders in purely the pejorative sense. The original thinker must endure periods of solitude and must expect to be misunderstood and perhaps bitterly opposed by peers. The ego must be strong to withstand these hardships.

While ordinarily we would consider *hubris* to be a negative trait, in the case of the explorer or innovator the above argument indicates that it may be an essential quality for success. One way to reconsider *hubris* is to put it in the context of our endowment by our Creator. That is, we may justifiably be arrogant in the sense of having great confidence in our abilities because these abilities were given to us by God.

God's greatest gift to man is that of intellect, or understanding . . . God gave this power to man that it might be used for the advancement of civilization, for the good of humanity, to increase love and concord and peace.[3]

Furthermore, we note that the creative impulse is a manifestation within us of the divine creative force by which the universe was created.

Whatever is in the heavens and whatever is on the earth is a direct evidence of the revelation within it of the attributes and names of God . . . To a supreme degree is this true of man, who, among all created things, hath been invested with the robe of such gifts . . . For in him are potentially revealed all the attributes and names of God to a degree that no other created being hath excelled or surpassed.[4]

Thus both our intellectual capacities and the urge to express them are gifts from God, not aberrations.

The key to the successful use of *hubris* is that it be tempered by humility. *Hubris* tempered by humility leads to a balanced type of confidence which we may perhaps label strength of character, for want of a better term. The difficulty here is that even if someone is truly humble, the mere fact that they are doing or attempting something great or difficult leads others to view them as arrogant or prideful out of jealousy. Many people resent the great sprinter Carl Lewis who has been able to state factually for over ten years that he is the fastest man on earth, as demonstrated by his several Olympic gold medals, and yet I have never heard him boast about his achievement or seen him act proudly. Thus those who dare to achieve greatness and challenge authority by discovering new things risk the labels of arrogance and pride due to the jealousy of others, even when the charge is unjustified.

Several considerations can help one achieve humility. First, one can, of course, make mistakes and thus must be careful not to state too strongly that one is right and others are wrong. Second, even if one is correct, the process of science is one that obliterates its own history. That is, most scientific discoveries and methods are eventually superseded by better, more precise, more comprehensive ones. In rapidly moving fields this can happen within a few years or less. One must dare to have a grand hypothesis but remember that it may well be soon forgotten. Invoking the Bahá'í principle of work as worship helps make this balance easier to achieve. If one has as a primary goal of one's work service to all humanity, then the product of one's labours becomes a gift to be given rather than a status symbol or a bid for immortality. When an individual desires success not merely for the sake of achievement but to show that he is really better than or superior to others, then this is the death of humility. Bahá'u'lláh reminds us of the folly of this desire:

Know ye not why We created you all from the same dust? That no one should exalt himself over the other. Ponder at all times in your hearts how ye were created. Since We have created you all from one same substance it is incumbent on you to be even as one soul, to walk with the same feet, eat with the same mouth and dwell in the same land, that from your inmost being, by your deeds and actions, the signs of oneness and the essence of detachment may be made manifest. Such is My counsel to you, O concourse of light! Heed ye this counsel that ye may obtain the fruit of holiness from the tree of wondrous glory.[5]

Failure to balance these factors properly is at the root of both under-achievement and barriers to progress in science. Lack of confidence leads to under-achivement because the scientist refuses to speculate. Without bold hypotheses, models and experiments one is reduced to plodding and measuring things. Such attitudes lead to a desire for absolute certainty and a tendency to dismiss anything new as 'mere speculation'. Failure to understand that the intellect is God's gift also leads to confusion between one's self-esteem and one's actual abilities. Those whose self-image is damaged by events in their lives or who feel themselves to be young and inexperienced will fail to take seriously their true level of talent. They will then not attempt the 'difficult' or important problems. But many scientific problems in retrospect are seen to have simple solutions or to have yielded in the end to pure persistence. Many of today's key scientific problems are as open to solution as more mundane problems with far less payoff. Thus the lack of *hubris* causes a great deal of under-achievement.

Hubris unbalanced by humility leads to several types of sins of excess. The most visible problem is what might be called the crackpot syndrome. When a brilliant and successful scientist becomes convinced of his own freedom from error or the certainty of his particular hypothesis, he can become immune to criticism or to contrary evidence. This leads to many endless rounds of debate because no amount of evidence is sufficient to change the mind of the fanatic.[6] A tricky aspect of evaluating particular cases is that many who seem to be crackpots at the time turn out later to be right. When Wegener proposed the idea of continental drift 80 years ago this must have seemed exceedingly crazy to his contemporaries (he was in fact vilified for his views) and yet he was essentially correct. There is a key difference between his behaviour and that of a crackpot, however: Wegener was not immune to criticism and fully acknowledged that a weakness of his theory was the lack of a mechanism by which continents might move. Thus we can see that he was ahead of his time, but not suffering from irrational adherence to his hypotheses. Darwin likewise was tenacious in his views but was also acutely aware of the mechanisms and facts which were lacking to establish his theory of evolution. Darwin in fact spent many years attempting to fill in the gaps in his theory. The extrapolation of these examples to other realms of endeavour is obvious; however, the farther one moves away from the hard sciences, the harder it may be to tell who is really a crackpot and who a visionary.

Far more common than the crackpot is the 'expert'. The expert has also forgotten all about humility and is very proud of the fact that he knows all about his chosen specialty. The expert criticizes new ideas because they contradict what we 'know' to be true. The expert is frequently also intolerant of those who intrude on his intellectual territory. Even worse, becoming an expert actively interferes with creativity and discovery. Why this contradiction? After all, it would seem that an expert has more tools at his or her disposal for solving problems. Interference with creativity occurs because in the process of learning a subject, a network of facts, assumptions and models is created. Once one thinks one understands something, it is linked up to an explanation and supporting ideas. This construct may not be true, but it comes to seem real nevertheless. As one becomes more of an expert, a larger and more complex network of facts and explanations accumulates and solidifies, making it difficult to entertain radically different ideas or to recognize new problems.[7] Humility constantly reminds us that the scientific certainty of yesterday will be completely toppled tomorrow; thus we should be ready at any moment to discard any piece of knowledge and start afresh.

How does one avoid becoming an 'expert'? Astrophysicist S. Chandrasekhar gave a remarkable television interview a few years ago. He led a scientific career notable for a rate of productivity that had not slowed down even in his seventies. When asked how he avoided the drop in creativity and productivity that plagues many scientists, he replied that approximately every seven years he took up a new topic. He found that he would run out of new ideas after working in an area for too long. This pattern led him to tackle such subjects as the dynamics of stellar systems, white dwarfs, relativity and radiative transfer. Although all these subjects are in astrophysics, they are different enough to present unique problems.

One need only turn to Darwin to find a truly remarkable example of the value of changing topics. He wrote books on the origin of coral atolls, the geology of South America, pollination of orchids, ecology of earthworms, evolution, human emotions, the taxonomy of the world's barnacles and movement in plants.[8] When he decided that a topic was interesting, he would delve into it in depth for a period of years, write up his results and move on. After his early books on geology, he only returned to the topic a few times during the remainder of his career. Studies have shown that a wide spectrum of interests is typical of highly creative scientists and helps account for their creativity.[9]

Thus on the one hand we are all created from the same dust and should not exalt ourselves over others. Failure to remember this causes a poison to invade any intellectual endeavour because it interferes with self-criticism and testing of one's ideas objectively against reality. On the other hand, we are justified in having confidence in our abilities which are God-given and reflect His attributes. The Bahá'í writings promise that we will achieve God's Kingdom; therefore the world's problems must be solvable, and solvable by us.

Detachment

A key to maintaining the proper balance between *hubris* (or confidence) and humility and avoiding the pitfalls inherent in any type of creative or innovative work is a spirit of detachment. Detachment is a rather alien concept in current western culture, which vaunts the self and personality above all else and which holds self-esteem as the highest good.

Detachment is an attitude that arises from the realization of several key spiritual truths. The first of these is that our worth in the sight of God is unrelated to our material attainments. It has always been the case that many of those who first follow the Prophets of God are devoid of wealth or position. What has distinguished them is their faith, devotion and service.

Second, it is crucial to realize what the truly important things in life are. Bahá'u'lláh tells us:

For every one of you his paramount duty is to choose for himself that on which no other may infringe and none usurp from him. Such a thing . . . is the love of God, could ye but perceive it.[10]

When one realizes that the most valuable things in life are faith, devotion and service to God and to mankind, then one is on the way to true detachment, because these most valuable things do not accrue from material success nor can they be taken away. They are entirely internal and are not subject to success or failure or the opinions of others. In science one's accomplishments and discoveries are quickly obliterated by new discoveries and better theories, so the ephemeral nature of material accomplishments is more obvious than in certain other fields of endeavour. Detachment can be enhanced by taking refuge within God's mighty covenant because this provides a measure of safety in a changing world. A final factor contributing to detachment is the recognition that any great intellectual or other gift (including wealth) is given by the grace of God. We did not create ourselves nor endow ourselves with powers. Furthermore, the reason we have been given these gifts is to serve God, not merely to exalt ourselves.

A spirit of detachment is a great gift in the pursuit of the creative solution of problems. One of the most important characteristics of creative individuals is independence of thought.[11] In order to be truly creative or innovative one needs first to have a mastery of the tools of the trade, but then one must go beyond what is known and create something new. Detachment enables one to recognize that the current state of knowledge is ephemeral and not fixed in stone. Furthermore, by removing excessive concern over the opinions of others, one's mind becomes free to consider new ideas clearly and on their own merits. New ideas are fragile and easily destroyed by premature criticism. Detachment leads to the kind of objectivity that can nurture truly original concepts.

Detachment is also a mighty shield against the slings and arrows that face the would-be innovator. As noted above, an imbalance in the confidence–humility dimension can seriously impair creativity. Detachment helps prevent the excessive 'humility' that keeps many from doing new or unusual work because they do not believe that they are capable of doing it. Keeping in mind that one's intellect is a gift from God, the purpose of which is to uncover the secrets of creation, helps dispel feelings of inadequacy that prevent one from attempting the 'impossible'. That is, one has a right to do great things without the attempt to do so necessarily indicating megalomania. In addition, detachment shields one from fear of failure and fear of criticism, the two big fears that cause many to shy away from the new or unusual. True innovators are bound to seem odd or to receive unwarranted criticism, and detachment can help deflect negative responses without the individual's needing to isolate himself or develop a bitter, defensive persona in response.

Conversely, detachment helps combat the rigidity, conservatism and know-it-all-ism that tempt the expert but kill innovation. When one bears in mind that the knowledge of even the most brilliant person is but a drop from the ocean of all knowledge, and that all around us the unknown far outweighs the known, the concept that one could ever truly 'know it all' or be an expert can be seen clearly as an exercise in self-delusion. The extreme forms of *hubris* that result from the identification of oneself as the owner of an idea (and thus the crackpot's refusal to change his mind) are likewise tempered by detachment. Not only does one see then that one's discoveries are not really due to one's own efforts (because one's very skill is God's gift), but one sees that these products of creativity do not belong to oneself at all. The external world we try to understand is God's creation and we are blessed to be able to uncover its secrets. But even more fundamentally, the products of our creativity are truly gifts of service to humankind. By them we may serve others in a most fundamental way. Once created, a scientific theory or fact belongs, not to the creator, but to the community of scientists and to humankind where it has ramifying results. The best scientists recognize this and are not concerned about the ultimate fate of their work, hoping mainly that it will play a part in scientific progress.

Tranquillity

In our increasingly frenetic world, tranquillity is a scarce commodity. It is not merely our nerves that suffer, however. Lack of place and time for reflection have an adverse impact on our spiritual lives. The need for outer tranquillity in the search for inner tranquillity has a long tradition in all religions and is institutionalized in various forms of religious retreats. What is not so well known is that inner tranquillity is also conducive to success in creative endeavours, including science. Consider the sport of orienteering in which one attempts to navigate across country using a map and compass. The winner of an orienteering race is rarely the swiftest runner, but the one who has his bearings. In science also it is crucial to have one's bearings. The ability to still the mind, to achieve a calm, reflective attitude can contribute significantly to innovation and creativity in science. This is because the most important and yet most difficult step in science is the formulation of truly original ideas. Yet good ideas typically start as urgings, hints, wisps, vapours, images or vague analogies. Only the rare individual has them pop up in a concrete form, ready to act on. More likely is it that the phantasm will need encouragement and the patience to watch it drift by at its own pace. A hurried, impatient, 'busy' person will not give these ideas sufficient play or attention and will tend to rush on to more 'productive' work. Whereas the painter typically works alone and is almost forced into some sort of meditative or introspective state, a state in which verbal modes of thought are suppressed, it is all too easy for the scientist to rush from seminar to lab to computer, and the phone is an all-too-frequent interruption. A frenetic pace is very detrimental to the formulation of complex thoughts and receptivity to nascent breakthroughs. To quote James D. Watson, co-discoverer of the structure of DNA, 'much of our success was due to the long uneventful periods when we walked the colleges or read the new books'.[12]

In a study of student problem-solving,[13] it was initially thought that the better students would be found to read a difficult problem faster and solve it faster. In fact, the good students took much longer to read the problem, because they were thinking about it, but then took less time to answer the questions or do the calculations. The poor students often were jumping ahead and solving the wrong problem. On simple problems there was little difference in performance. In science also this habit of jumping ahead can lead to solving the wrong problem. The pace of academic life and research has become so frenetic that activity and motion have come to replace thought. The need for careful thought and planning is particularly acute for studies of complex systems where laboratory technique does not dominate, such as epidemiology, ecology and psychology. There is a simple test for freneticism: merely ask, 'Why am I collecting these data?' If you are too busy to answer or cannot explain it, the ratio of thought to activity is too low.

A technique for promoting deep contemplation is walking. This technique is looked down on today as being too low-tech. Besides, someone walking is obviously not working. Darwin used to take an hour's walk every day around a course he had laid out. He would become engrossed in his thoughts; therefore he put some small stones at the start, kicking one off at each round so that he did not have to keep track of how many circuits he had made or worry about time. It was during these walks that he wrestled with the deepest questions.

The practice of taking long walks as an intellectual activity used to be common in academic life in Europe. Professors would take their students on walks to debate, discuss and question. These days students are lucky even to see their professor in the halls. Our idea of a walk today is going to the copy machine. Some psychologists have found that taking patients for a walk is very effective in getting them to open up and express themselves. With our short attention spans these days, it would no doubt require practice to be able to come to conclusions or formulate complex thoughts while walking and remember them back in the office, but it can be done and would be beneficial.

Tranquillity, however, is more than just a technique such as walking or the safety of a remote office, free from phone calls. One can take a quiet walk in a remote wood yet still find one's mind racing with thoughts and anxieties. True tranquillity is brought about by the cultivation of certain key attitudes. First among these is detachment. Constant dwelling on getting the Nobel Prize or getting that next promotion poisons the intuition and receptivity to new and subtle ideas. The realization of the smallness of even the greatest of our accomplishments allows one to maintain a degree of emotional distance from the work at hand so that the needs of the work itself, rather than our hopes and wishes, provide the guidance for how to proceed. Detachment also allows ideas to enter our consciousness which may contradict our previous results (and perhaps contradict our cherished hopes), which a busy and emotional mind will suppress or ignore but which are crucial to correcting one's course.

Second, the Arabic phrase 'inshallah' (God willing) is relevant. The realization that the everyday problems that surround us or the fate of a particular experiment are not totally under our control but may be subject to God's plan causes us to say, 'I will solve this problem, God willing.' This frees one from the anxiety caused by believing that everything is on one's shoulders. Furthermore, many discoveries in science do in fact happen by chance, thus whether one will be lucky today is to an extent at God's mercy. Clearly this should not be carried so far that one fails to put forth serious effort while waiting for divine inspiration or attributes a lucky break to direct divine intervention.

Finally, in order to bring tranquillity to one's work, it is helpful to cultivate it in a purer context: that of spiritual devotion. The devotional attitude experienced during meditation and prayer is a com- mingling of focus on the other, losing oneself in something larger, something eternal, and the feeling of a sense of the divine purpose (among other things). Having experienced these feelings in a devotional context, it is possible to transfer them to the context of creative problem-solving.

Honesty

One might not think of honesty as relevant to creativity in science, but in my experience prominent creative scientists are quite honest, both with them- selves and with others. Note that this is not necessarily true of all prominent scientists, because some reach prominence on the basis of the labours of sub- ordinates or by being prolific at the expense of being innovative. Why might this quality of honesty be important? After all, research has never been considered a domain for ethical difficulties such as we encounter in medicine or business. The reason is that if one is successfully to confront Nature and discern her secrets, absolute lack of self-deception is required. One can deceive the customer, bluff in sports and bully in business, but Nature cannot be tricked. When one conducts an experiment, the outcome is not influenced at all by one's bluffing or charm or good looks. On the contrary, self-deception is devastating in the context of interpreting experiments. There is a natural psychological tendency to seek evidence that confirms what we already believe and to ignore evidence that contradicts our beliefs.[14] Conducting an experiment that can only confirm what we already believe is useful as a check on knowledge acquired by others but it does not lead to scientific progress. Thus one must constantly ask oneself, 'Am I interpreting this experiment according to my preferences or am I really seeing what is there?' Failure to be honest can lead to tragic consequences. For example, a prominent turn-of-the-century geologist became convinced in his later years that all rocks were fossil deposits of aquatic micro-organisms. His self-deception was so complete that no matter what he looked at under the poor quality microscope of that day, he saw microfossils. During the last years of his life no one would publish his work because it was so obviously biased and immune from criticism.

It is well to remember that slightly crazy ideas are crucial in science. The wild analogy or model is often useful or even correct. Those who become passionate advocates of such ideas are not necessarily deceiving themselves, however. It is instructive to examine how such people deal with facts contrary to their beliefs. When the first experiments testing Einstein's theories seemed to contradict them, Einstein insisted the experiments were wrong. He had reason to be sceptical because of the power of his theory and the difficulty of the experiments. Consider the case of Pasteur.[15] He had a set of grand hypotheses or goals that in retrospect we can see to be not only wrong but a little crazy. For example, he dreamed of creating left-handed organisms (constituted from chirally left-handed organic chemicals) and thus become famous for creating a new form of life. In attempting to prove his theories he came upon many experimental results that were not what he expected or what he was looking for. He had the honesty (or perhaps objectivity) to confront these results for what they were and publish them. Other scientists of his day had actually observed many of the same phenomena but failed to believe them because they contradicted what they already knew. Thus in the case of Pasteur his honesty saved him from becoming a crackpot (though, of course, he was not a saint nor even always honest). It is thus clearly important to be honest with the facts and not let one's biases lead to self-deception. No one is ever free of biases, but honesty about their existence can prevent their negative effects.

Science is a good educator in honesty because one is more frequently forced to own up to any attempted deceptions by the uncompromising nature of the real world, in sharp contrast to other parts of one's life.

Service

A key to the achievement of all of the beneficial attitudes discussed above is an attitude of service. In the Bahá'í teachings, all work performed in the spirit of service is considered to be worship, but this is especially so of creative work.

> ... in accordance with the divine teachings the acquisition of sciences and the perfection of arts are considered acts of worship. If a man engageth with all his power in the acquisition of a science or in the perfection of an art, it is as if he has been worshipping God in the churches and temples ... What bounty greater than this that science should be considered as an act of worship and art as service to the Kingdom of God.[16]

The development of arts and sciences is the means by which civilization progresses. The progress of civilization, by providing the material means for universal education and the basis for a lawful and orderly society, is essential for the spiritual upliftment of the individual. Bahá'u'lláh asserts that the Prophets are the source for much of the progress we have observed throughout history.

> The light which these souls radiate is responsible for the progress of the world and the advancement of its people. They ... constitute the animating force through which the arts and wonders of the world are made manifest.[17]

Thus one's creative acts have a serious spiritual dimension. By viewing one's work in the context of service and the progress of civilization, it becomes much easier to maintain a spiritual balance between *hubris* and humility, to gain detachment, and to achieve tranquillity. In this context, one does one's work less for applause or profit and more to please God.

A ramification of achieving an attitude of service and worship in one's work is its effect on one's spiritual growth. One's growth depends on service because it is only by deeds that one can actually manifest these qualities. This is why service is emphasized in the Bahá'í Faith: if we wait to be perfect Bahá'ís before we arise to aid His cause we will never be able to arise. The very process of arising makes us worthy and causes our growth. This is why monasticism is not practised by Bahá'ís. Whereas a mother of small children is constantly called upon to render service, as are those in many walks of life, the creative act tends to be a solitary one. Scientists and artists spend a great deal of time alone with their own thoughts. The benefit of the work to others is not immediate or close at hand. By remembering that such work is worship and performing it in a spirit of service, the creative person becomes reconnected to the life of humankind and the progress of civilization. This has a profoundly beneficial effect, not only by instilling positive attitudes, as discussed above, but also by helping to guide one's work away from the trivial or negative.

As acts of service, creative work can become a vehicle for the spiritual progress of the individual. Successfully to pursue creative endeavours in a spirit of service, one must overcome many negative

influences and grow spiritually to a degree not called
for in many professions. Pursuit of creative work is
thus a great gift, a great test and a great opportunity.

Science as a Calling

It is possible to see one's work in science not merely
as a job but as a calling. The sense of awe and
wonder at Nature's mysteries is a glimpse of the
divine awe felt by Moses at the burning bush. For
when we first set foot on the moon, uncover the
secrets of the atom, and recreate the life of the
dinosaurs, we catch a glimpse of the hand of God
Himself and His power and glory. Establishing a
connection to the divine mystery in this way is a key
step along the path to the Friend. In addition, a
creative life of science is potentially a path to
spiritual growth and a vehicle for service to humankind. These three ingredients – a sense of the
numinous, a process of growth and service – are the
requisites for recognizing science as potentially a
true calling. We may extend this conclusion to other
fields of creative endeavour as well.

Conclusion

I hope to have demonstrated that how one works is
not unrelated to one's spiritual condition. Not only
do spiritual qualities enhance problem-solving, creativity and productivity even in practical fields such
as science, it is doubtful if one's full capacity can be
achieved in any other way. Furthermore, serious
dangers await those brilliant minds who attempt to

scale great intellectual heights without the protection of humility, detachment, honesty and a spirit of service. How far the mighty can fall has been a recurring theme of literature and biography. By taking a spiritual approach to creative endeavours, we risk less and can achieve more than we would otherwise dare to imagine.

Connection to God
spiritual growth
service to humanity
7 true calling

4

Evolution in Bahá'í Perspective*

As science has advanced, it has increasingly come into conflict with religion. The history of active conflict goes back to the Middle Ages. Almost every aspect of science was initially opposed by the Church, particularly astronomy, geology and medicine.[1] Galileo, for example, was forced to recant. While in earlier periods religion had the upper hand, including the power to ban books and imprison heretics, today science has the upper hand and sits in harsh judgement of religion. The ordinary person sees the evidence of the power and authority of science every day. Consequently, if some aspect of religion seems to clash directly with a scientific principle, there is a tendency to reject religion outright. This conflict is most evident in the case of evolution. The theory of evolution does not merely shake the certainty that the Bible is literally true by contradicting Genesis; it attacks the foundation of religion itself. If the Adam

*Copyright © 1990, Association for Bahá'í Studies. All rights reserved. Permission to reprint this article has been granted by the Association for Bahá'í Studies in whose *Journal* it appeared in its original form in April 1990 under the title of 'On Human Origins: A Bahá'í Perspective'.

and Eve story is wrong and we evolved, then it would seem that God did not create us; we are nothing special and in fact it is pure chance that we are here at all. This contradicts the whole theme of religion that the world was created for a purpose and that life has meaning. Furthermore, if we are just one species of animal, then it seems exceedingly unlikely that any divine power is guiding our destiny. As animals, we would also be unlikely to have a soul, an essential component of Christian theology. While some compromise positions have been attempted, the result is a watering down of Christianity that takes the passion and certainty out of it.

Introduction

There is no real resolution to the dilemma posed by evolution within the context of mainstream Christianity and as a consequence many have turned away from religion. It is interesting that the primary aspect of science actively resisted or denied today by those who are religious is the theory of evolution and the evolutionary explanation of human origins. In surveys of adults or even college students, a substantial minority and sometimes even a majority do not accept scientific accounts of the origin of the universe, life and humanity. These people state that they accept the biblical version of origins as literally true.

Active attacks on evolution continue today in the United States in the state school arena with 'creation science' and attempts to remove evolution from textbooks. Particularly disturbing are blatant distortions of scientific method and evidence, especially in evolution and geology (documented and refuted in Strahler's *Science and Earth History:* The Evolution/ Creation Controversy). For example, some claim that the vast deposits of bones of prehistoric animals found in geologic strata were all laid down in Noah's flood and represent animals that did not make it onto the ark. It is asserted that the bones of early hominids that have been found were actually put there by the devil to confound us. The response from scientists is equally vigorous, resulting in a heated debate in the scientific and popular literature.[2] Scientists have also mounted attacks on religion in general and claim to prove that God does not exist.[3]

A brief explanation of the theory of evolution helps to clarify the roots of the conflict. The theory of evolution as currently understood is based on a set of well-tested premises and extensive data.[4]

- The morphology, physiology and behaviour of all organisms is determined by their genetic code, stored in DNA, interacting with environmental factors.

- When genetic information is passed to the next generation, transmission is not perfect. Recombination mixes the traits of the parents. Information is lost or altered via mutations, deletions, inversions, chromosome doubling and other mechanisms.

- Natural selection acts on organisms via differential survival and fecundity, favouring those traits best adapted to the circumstances that the organism must face (e.g. climate, predators).

- Chance effects influence the course of evolution, particularly via extinctions.

When we trace our earliest ancestors back several million years, Africa appears to be the cradle of both ancient and modern forms.[5] While very primitive humans (*Homo erectus* and later Neanderthal) spread out from Africa to Europe and Asia over a million years ago, modern humans arose in Africa about 200,000 years ago.[6] About 100,000 years ago modern humans spread out from Africa in a great wave and supplanted (and perhaps mixed with) pre-existing early humans in Europe and Asia.[7] This date thus represents the beginning of the worldwide spread of humanity and the earliest date for racial differentiation. Such a recent origin for the races means that most racial differences are rather superficial and trivial.[8]*

The period around 10,000 years ago represents a unique crisis and turning point in human history. During the period 12,000 to 10,000 BP, rapid global warming caused the final retreat of the global ice sheets of the last glaciation. This rapid warming was accompanied by massive shifts in local climates and vegetation such as expansion of the grasslands in the American West. Animals previously adapted to cold climates, particularly larger mammals, were unable to adapt and many became extinct. By 10,000 BP the

---

*Interestingly, the oldest remains of modern humans outside of Africa are dated 92,000 years BP from Mount Carmel, Israel (see Stringer, 'Eden'; Valladas et al., 'Dating'), the location of the world administrative centre of the Bahá'í Faith.

large mammal herds in most areas outside Africa, upon which early humans had depended, were either reduced in number or extinct. We can think of this time as the historical expulsion from the Garden, in a sense. This crisis forced people into developing new food sources including fishing, more sophisticated hunting techniques and agriculture,[9] thus leading directly to the establishment of more advanced culture and technology. In particular, the earliest dates known for the domestication of both plants and animals are in the period 12,000–10,000 BP in the Middle East.[10] The period around 10,000 BP is when the earliest villages (permanent settlements) were established, also in the Middle East.

While it is *a priori* not goal-directed, evolution has tended to produce, particularly in mammals and birds, more elaborate sensory modes, greater homeostatic control of physiology, increased care of young and larger brains because these traits enhance survival. We humans are the beneficiaries of these trends. This evolutionary progression is marvellous to behold and full of small miracles, but the concept that we arose by a purely physical process is anathema to many because it removes purposefulness from the universe. It leaves a watch without a watchmaker, a body without a soul, a universe with no meaning or order or feeling. Thus, the part of evolution attacked most vehemently has to do with human origins and the origins of the universe, i.e. with God as Creator. Even Wallace, co-discoverer with Darwin of evolution, maintained that everything had evolved except human beings, who were a special creation.

In place of faith, some attempt to find ethical roots

in evolution itself. By understanding the way in which humanity evolved socially and genetically, they hope to discover a basis for social order and ethics. In the tendency for evolution to create more complex forms,[11] they seek a general organizing principle (complexity, integration, system, world-mind) from which moral imperatives can be derived.[12] As we will see later, such ideas though incomplete are not completely incompatible with Bahá'í belief. Some have used the principles of natural selection (the 'selfish gene') as a basis for the guidance of society.[13] Unfortunately, the 'selfish gene' provides only very limited guidance on ethics (e.g. it is not adaptive to kill your relatives) and almost none on larger social issues. Wilson[14] (*Biophilia*), as another example, argues that we are genetically evolved to have an attraction or affinity to all forms of life. Most of these writers seek to replace the (to them) outmoded social order based on religion with one based on the guidance inspired by evolution. While the above-cited authors tend to view evolution in terms that lead to the derivation of humanistic values, such need not be the case. Social Darwinism and Monism, as propounded by Ernst Haeckel and other German philosophers of the nineteenth century,[15] reflected a world view that applied the struggle for existence logically to human society, with the struggle being between nations (races). The superior race, the Aryans, was seen to have a right to take land away from inferior peoples. Exterminating the 'lesser' races, the old, the ill or the deformed was not viewed as criminal but as a matter of racial hygiene. This rationale was explicitly incorporated

into Nazism and carried out with horrible consequences.[16] Evolution *per se* is thus an insufficient
basis for a human moral order. The problem with
extrapolating from Nature's order to human society
is that multiple moral codes are compatible with
Nature, many of which lead to societies in which few
of us would willingly live.

If evolution and religion were marriage partners,
we would be tempted to diagnose 'irreconcilable
differences' and grant them the divorce they both
seem to seek. However, the consequences of admit-
ting failure here is, as we have seen, mental turmoil
and massive loss of faith. Furthermore, both evolution and religion claim to embody solutions to the
same set of moral and social issues. Medicine can
extend life but reduces its meaning. Psychology
claims hegemony over understanding our behaviour
but is powerless to give us values and comes to
absurd conclusions like 'open marriage' being healthy.
Where is the solution to this conflict?

What is needed is a synthesis within which religion
is compatible with evolution, without creating pseudo-
religions, such as social Darwinism or secular humanism.
Such a synthesis is not only possible but has already
been achieved in the Bahá'í Faith.

Science and God's Existence

Before specifically dealing with evolution and human
origins, it is necessary to clarify the Bahá'í views on
science. It is a fundamental, central teaching of the
Bahá'í Faith that science and religion are in harmony. The Bahá'í Faith emphatically and explicitly

accepts scientific accounts of the creation of the universe, our planet and life on earth. The current scientific explanation[17] is that the known universe began as a fireball (the Big Bang) 10 to 20 billion years ago and that our solar system formed from the dust of space much later. At the instant of creation, all original matter was concentrated at a single point, or singularity, of unimaginable heat and density, which then exploded outward and gradually cooled. What happened 'before' this time is unknown. Some would argue that 'before' the Big Bang has no meaning because time did not even exist then. Although the Bahá'í writings specify that God has neither a beginning nor an ending, Bahá'u'lláh states the following regarding 'the beginning of creation':

. . . this is a matter on which conceptions vary by reason of the divergences in men's thoughts and opinions. Wert thou to assert that it hath ever existed and shall continue to exist, it would be true; or wert thou to affirm the same concept as is mentioned in the sacred Scriptures, no doubt would there be about it, for it hath been revealed by God, the Lord of the worlds . . . His creation had ever existed beneath His shelter from the beginning that hath no beginning, apart from its being preceded by a Firstness which cannot be regarded as firstness and originated by a Cause inscrutable even unto all men of learning.

That which hath been in existence had existed before, but not in the form thou seest today. The world of existence came into being through the heat generated from the interaction between the active force and that which is its recipient. These two are the same, yet they are different.[18]

Note that this passage was written in the late nine-teenth century, before any hint of our current concepts of cosmology. 'Abdu'l-Bahá refers to the gradual process of the formation of the earth.[19] Bahá'u'lláh specifically dismissed literal interpretations of the Bible that give the age of the earth as between 5,000 and 6,000 years:

> The learned men, that have fixed at several thousand years the life of this earth, have failed, throughout the long period of their observation, to consider either the number or the age of the other planets.[20]

He goes on to state:

> Know thou that every fixed star hath its own planets, and every planet its own creatures, whose number no man can compute.[21]

Note that these statements were made prior to 1890, when few scientists accepted either a great age for the earth or the existence of other planets with life. Life on at least a few other planets outside our solar system is now viewed by many scientists as almost inevitable.[22] The origin of life on earth as simple organisms with subsequent evolution to higher forms (discussed further below) is granted in the Bahá'í writings.[23] There is also no quarrel with the fossil record. No claim is made that prehuman bones were placed there by the 'devil' to confound us, as claimed by 'creation scientists'. Bahá'ís do not accept rein-carnation and do not emphasize miracles as a basis for faith. The Bahá'í writings on the topics of greatest conflict between science and religion, there-fore, are not in conflict with science.

To be compatible with science, religion should be internally consistent and its predictions should be accurate. There are false and unscientific disciplines, such as astrology, which can explain everything but predict nothing. 'Abdu'l-Bahá explained many times that religion is logical and can be studied using the tools of logic. In this context, a religious account of human origins must be both internally consistent and consistent with science. It is important first of all to clarify the Bahá'í view of causation. 'Abdu'l-Bahá states that events in the world may have three causes: necessary, accidental and voluntary.[24] Necessary causes include the law of gravity, laws of physics and other laws that operate in a regular, predictable way. A necessary property is one which is fundamentally a part of that thing: 'the inherent property of a thing can in no wise be dissociated from it'.[25] A very clear example of such a property is gravity. Any object with mass will attract other objects to it according to a fixed relationship. It is not possible to separate gravity from an object and have an object without gravity. These laws are manifestations of God's purpose in that God established these laws, but they operate independently of active divine intervention. Accidental relationships or properties or events in our modern terminology are not without cause but are unpredictable. Examples include throwing a die, the exact spot that a leaf falling from a tree will land, where lightning will strike, etc. These things have causes, but the causes are so complicated and unobservable that we say that they are random or stochastic. This is what I mean by a chance event. Voluntary causes are those attributable to free agents able to exercise their will, such as human beings.

Bahá'u'lláh gives an explanation of fate and chance in the following:

Know thou, O fruit of My Tree, that the decrees of the Sovereign Ordainer, as related to fate and predestination, are of two kinds. Both are to be obeyed and accepted. The one is irrevocable, the other is, as termed by men, impending. To the former all must unreservedly submit, inasmuch as it is fixed and settled. God, however, is able to alter or repeal it. As the harm that must result from such a change will be greater than if the decree had remained unaltered, all, therefore, should willingly acquiesce in what God hath willed and confidently abide by the same.

The decree that is impending, however, is such that prayer and entreaty can succeed in averting it.[26]

'Abdu'l-Bahá elaborates on this:

Fate is of two kinds: one is decreed, and the other is conditional or impending. The decreed fate is that which cannot change or be altered, and conditional fate is that which may occur. So, for this lamp, the decreed fate is that the oil burns and will be consumed; therefore, its eventual extinction is a decree which it is impossible to alter or to change because it is a decreed fate. In the same way, in the body of man a power of life has been created, and as soon as it is destroyed and ended, the body will certainly be decomposed, so when the oil in this lamp is burnt and finished, the lamp will undoubtedly become extinguished.

But conditional fate may be likened to this: while there is still oil, a violent wind blows on the lamp, which extinguishes it. This is a conditional fate. It is wise to avoid it, to protect oneself from it, to be cautious and circumspect.[27]

These quotations apparently support the concept that chance or accident exists in the world. The existence of chance or accident does not invalidate the inevitability of large-scale predestined events such as the occurrence of a Prophet and the triumph of His cause, however.

The third type of causation is voluntary, of which divine Will is an instance. In earlier periods, divine Will was popularly assumed to be responsible for the fall of every leaf and drop of rain, and individuals were considered to be largely subject to fate. In the Bahá'í view, such detailed manipulation of the natural world by God violates the existence of free will in humans, upon which our spiritual progress depends: without free will we cannot choose to do good and therefore cannot be held accountable for doing evil.[28] The necessity for free will leads inevitably to the existence of an imperfect world.[29] God intervenes only to further the goal of humanity's cultural evolution. God's Will operates according to its own set of divine laws and manifests itself particularly clearly in the person of the Prophet and in the events that surround Him. Divine Will is popularly perceived as producing 'miracles', but it is also manifest in terms of revelation, dreams, visions and coincidences. Such events surround the person of the Prophet and propel religious events forward. As noted above, although divine Will is a force that operates in the world today and can affect individual lives, not everything that happens can be called God's Will; nor are we as individuals necessarily privileged to know which events are part of God's plan.

Human Evolution

Having explained the Bahá'í concept of causation and law, I now return to the issue of human evolution. In the Bahá'í view, humanity did not merely evolve accidently, but rather it was God's purpose for creation that humanity should arise.[30] Humanity's origin can be viewed as the unfolding of God's Plan. 'Abdu'l-Bahá uses the analogy of a seed holding within it the potential of the tree. Similarly, the earliest life contained the potential for humanity, though not in the sense of a mere unfolding, as in the earlier view of the homunculus curled up in the sperm cell. Geneticists discredited this view years ago because of the role of chance in evolution.[31] Evolution is influenced by three major components of chance: chance mutations, chance extinctions and chance migrations. Humanity was thus not pre-ordained in a programmed manner because any one of hundreds of chance events could have deflected the path actually taken by human evolution.

The Bahá'í view is not that the earliest life literally had a step-by-step plan for evolution but rather that it contained the potentialities that unfolded because of evolution, which, as has often been remarked, tends gradually to produce higher, more complex forms. In this view, the unfolding of higher forms by degrees is the way that God works. Individuals, cultures, species, knowledge and individual intelligences must all go through a process of development. As 'Abdu'l-Bahá states:

For the supreme organization of God, and the universal natural system, surround all beings, and all are subject to this rule. When you consider this universal system, you see that there is not one of the beings which at its coming into existence has reached the limit of perfection. No, they gradually grow and develop, and then attain the degree of perfection.[32]

In specific reference to Darwinian evolution, 'Abdu'l-Bahá states:

Moses taught that the world was brought into existence in the six days of creation. This is an allegory, a symbolic form of the ancient truth that the world evolved gradually. Darwin can refer to Moses for his theory of evolution. God did not allow the world to come into existence all at once, rather the divine breath of life manifested itself in the commanding Word of God, Logos, which engendered and begot the world. We thus have a progressive process of creation, and not a one-time happening. Moses' days of creation represent time spans of millions of years. From Pythagoras to ibn-i-Síná (known as Avicenna) to the 'faithful brothers from Basra', through Darwin and to the blessed manifestions of the Báb and Bahá'u'lláh, both scholars and Prophets have testified to the progressive creative action of the Logos (divine breath of life). The Darwinian and monistic theories of evolution and the origin of species are not materialistic, atheistic ideas; they are religious truths which the godless and the deluded have unjustifiably used in their campaign against religion and the Bible.[33]

A more elaborate explication of this view is given by 'Abdu'l-Bahá:

. . . it is evident that this terrestrial globe, having once found existence, grew and developed in the matrix of the universe, and came forth in different forms and conditions, until gradually it attained this present perfection, and became adorned with innumerable beings, and appeared as a finished organization.

Then it is clear that original matter, which is in the embryonic state, and the mingled and composed elements which were its earliest forms, gradually grew and developed during many ages and cycles, passing from one shape and form to another, until they appeared in this perfection, this system, this organization and this establishment, through the supreme wisdom of God.

Let us return to our subject that man, in the beginning of his existence and in the womb of the earth, like the embryo in the womb of the mother, gradually grew and developed, and passed from one form to another, from one shape to another, until he appeared with this beauty and perfection, this force and this power. It is certain that in the beginning he had not this loveliness and grace and elegance, and that he only by degrees attained this shape, this form, this beauty and this grace. There is no doubt that the human embryo did not at once appear in this form: neither did it then become the manifestation of the words 'Blessed, therefore, be God, the most excellent of Makers'. Gradually it passed through various conditions and different shapes, until it attained this

form and beauty, this perfection, grace and loveliness. Thus it is evident and confirmed that the
development and growth of man on this earth, until
he reached his present perfection, resembled the
growth and development of the embryo in the womb
of the mother: by degrees it passed from condition
to condition, from form to form, from one shape to
another, for this is according to the requirement of
the universal system and Divine Law.[34]

A significant remaining question is whether human
beings may be viewed as a special creation. The
Bahá'í view is both yes and no. Yes, because humanity was in the eye of God from the beginning, and He
created us; no, because we progressed through various forms rather than being created in one moment
from clay. As 'Abdu'l-Bahá explains:

> Let us suppose that there was a time when man
> walked on his hands and feet, or had a tail; this
> change and alteration is like that of the foetus in the
> womb of the mother. Although it changes in all ways,
> and grows and develops until it reaches the perfect
> form, from the beginning it is a special species . . .
> To recapitulate: as man in the womb of the mother
> passes from form to form, from shape to shape,
> changes and develops, and is still the human species
> from the beginning of the embryonic period – in the
> same way man, from the beginning of his existence in
> the matrix of the world, is also a distinct species –
> that is, man – and has gradually evolved from one
> form to another. Therefore, this change of appear-
> ance, this evolution of members, this development
> and growth, even though we admit the reality of
> growth and progress [i.e. if we admit, for example,
> that man had formerly been a quadruped, or had had

a tail], does not prevent the species from being original. Man from the beginning was in this perfect form and composition, and possessed capacity and aptitude for acquiring material and spiritual perfections, and was the manifestation of these words, 'We will make man in Our image and likeness'. He has only become more pleasing, more beautiful and more graceful. Civilization has brought him out of his wild state, just as the wild fruits which are cultivated by a gardener become finer, sweeter and acquire more freshness and delicacy.[35]

It is perhaps not easy to understand how human beings can be a special creation and still have evolved. This is a subtle concept. A further quotation from 'Abdu'l-Bahá helps clarify this.

The reflection of the divine perfections appears in the reality of man, so he is the representative of God, the messenger of God. If man did not exist, the universe would be without result, for the object of existence is the appearance of the perfections of God.

Therefore, it cannot be said there was a time when man was not. All that we can say is that this terrestrial globe at one time did not exist, and at its beginning man did not appear upon it. But from the beginning which has no beginning, to the end which has no end, a Perfect Manifestation always exists. This Man of Whom we speak is not every man; we mean the Perfect Man. For the noblest part of the tree is the fruit, which is the reason of its existence. If the tree had no fruit, it would have no meaning.[36]

Some Answered Questions

A final note is needed on understanding 'Abdu'l-Bahá's discussions of human evolution. *Some Answered*

Questions, quoted in large measure above, was recorded from verbal answers given to a Bahá'í pilgrim, Laura Clifford Barney, during the years 1904–6. Parts of 'Abdu'l-Bahá's answers appear contradictory but upon closer inspection are not. For example, at one point 'Abdu'l-Bahá argues that the possession of vestigial organs does not prove the absence of special creation but concludes the discussion by stating that humans have passed through various forms. It seems clear that 'Abdu'l-Bahá is using a pedagogical device here. He is refuting the principal arguments of materialists so as to break the questioner out of any confining notions or preconceived ideas, thus allowing His explanation to be effectively heard and understood. The introduction to the book notes that 'Abdu'l-Bahá is more pedagogical here than in His other works. Quoting single sentences out of the context of the entire passage could thus be construed as opposing evolution, which is not the case. In the above section, I have therefore focused on His concluding paragraphs to the individual sections, in which He presents His final arguments. In addition, I have used extended quotations to preserve context and meaning.

From the above discussion we see that the Bahá'í view is inherently and fundamentally evolutionary. Biological evolution, individual development and cultural advancement are all aspects of one fundamental process. This is how God has ordained the world to work. Evolution is thus not in conflict with religion, rather, it is at the very heart of God's purpose and way of working. This is a fundamentally new view of the very nature of religion, in distinct contrast to the static world views and philosophies of the past.

We can recognize, therefore, three components in human origins. First, the lawlike component of evolution gradually leads to higher forms. More recent, advanced organisms tend to have larger brains, greater internal homeostasis and more advanced sensory abilities and adaptive behaviours. Larger brains increase the chances of survival and lengthen lifespan. Second, chance leads to random variations (e.g. many of the randomly derived differences among individuals) and random origins and extinctions. Third, I postulate (the Bahá'í writings do not specify this) that divine Will may have operated at times to help guide the process towards humanity; it was God's intention from the beginning that humanity should arise. In this view, the same mode of action for God is postulated to have acted in the past as acts today; that is, subtle interventions that further God's Plan of an advancing civilization for humanity. Thus, God's role in human origins is one of a periodic intervenor in the natural process of development of higher forms called biological evolution. This is a plausible explanation: if you believe, from faith or evidence, that God is active in our world today as Bahá'ís believe He is, then God's role in human origins can be seen as consistent with that belief.

However, the role of chance in evolution is such a fundamental one that it leads to a scientific argument against God's very existence and thus it requires further examination here. The conflict between the existence of chance and God's purpose for man can be resolved as follows. All religions give humanity as the reason for the existence of the world: God created the world so that we could inhabit it; He created us to know Him. Thus, a fundamental premise of all religion is that if humans did not exist, then there would be no reason for the world to exist, and God's purpose would be unfulfilled. This line of reasoning runs into difficulty with the nature of the evolutionary process. Since there is a very high chance for something adverse to have happened to our ancestors (i.e. extinction), and since given a minutely different course of events we would look different, there is nothing to suggest that we followed any predestined course to arrive here in the twentieth century appearing just as we do (since we are supposedly made in 'God's image'). Thus, there is no 'purpose' in life and God does not exist. There is no resolution to this puzzle in the context of earlier religions, but there is in the context of the Bahá'í teachings. Current theology is too concrete and focuses on external appearances. Since we are made in God's image, artists depict angels that look like us (though usually blond). 'Abdu'l-Bahá states, however, that external appearances are of no consequence whatsoever. Thus, racial differences are meaningless from a spiritual perspective. It is our minds, our rational souls that distinguish us and enable us to know God. Thus, if we had evolved differently and looked different, it would be of no consequence to our spiritual state.

While the exact path followed by human evolution is an improbable one, the evolution of sentient beings is not so improbable.[37] There was a dinosaur

(Stenonychosaurus) that was bipedal, had opposable
thumbs, and was quite intelligent for its type.[38] That
path could have led to 'humans'. In our own history,
there were several pre-human hominids that could
have evolved further had they survived. The pygmy
chimpanzee walks upright frequently and has much
greater language capacity than the regular chimp or
other apes. Who is to say that we could not be
replaced by it if we destroy ourselves? The Bahá'í
writings refer to other planets and other creatures and
include them in God's Plan. When we consider the
infinitude of stars in the sky, if even a small percent-
age have planets with life, then sentient beings
capable of knowing God are virtually inevitable. By
'Abdu'l-Bahá's definition, they would still be 'in the
image of God', because the rational soul or intelligence is the distinguishing feature of 'humans'. If
God exists, it is probable that these beings have their
own Prophets, just as we do. Thus, we can conclude
that the universe can have a purpose and that we are
part of that purpose, even though chance does play a
major role. In addition, as mentioned above, there
may have been direct intervention by God in the
evolutionary process.

Another aspect of this issue of chance conflicting
with a divine Plan is the conflict with free will. If we
have free will, then again it seems that there is no
possibility for the existence of an overall plan.
However, our free will is always constrained.[39] Consider the soldier in battle. The commanders have
made plans and arrayed their forces but each soldier
still can be a hero or a coward within that context. In
the same way, both free will and chance are com-

ponents of causation but their existence does not rule out the existence of a grand scheme.

Understanding our biological origins still leaves us with a riddle, for if we trace our ancestors back in time they become by degrees more primitive. At what point in this succession do we begin to see self-consciousness, higher-level thought and other functions that are indicative of the rational mind? More specifically, at what point can we say that there is a soul? All the major religions are founded upon the supposition of a human soul, and if we only differ from the animals by degrees, then either we do not have a soul or other animals also have a soul.

While I cannot prove that other animals do not have a soul, it is the basic assumption of Christianity, Islam and the Bahá'í Faith, at least, that human beings differ from animals in the possession of an immortal, higher, moral self: the soul. Such an assumption is not subject to proof. For the purpose of this paper, it is sufficient to ask whether this assumption can be reconciled with our acceptance of an evolutionary origin for humanity.

'Abdu'l-Bahá's solution to this problem begins with an analogy.[40] Consider the foetus in the womb. It goes through various forms, at one point having gills, at another a tail. Yet throughout these stages it is a human infant and has a soul since, in the Bahá'í view, the soul exists from conception. In the same way, human beings went through various forms throughout the evolutionary process but were still human, with a soul, from the beginning. God had a purpose for humanity and gave a special blessing to all our ancestors. As we go farther back in time to more primitive forms, the soul becomes more veiled, undeveloped and less realized, but it still exists. Thus humanity is simultaneously a special creation and a product of evolution, different from animals in kind through possession of a soul but linked to the animals by lineage and physical attributes.

The above view represents, as best I can reconstruct it, the Bahá'í view of human origins in terms of God's Plan. It is neither a mathematical proof nor a laboratory study, and only further elaboration will fill in all the details. What it does offer, I hope, is a plausible middle ground between mental compartmentalization on the one hand and a choice between atheism and fanaticism on the other.

In conclusion, in the context of the Bahá'í teachings it is possible to take both a religious view of evolution without altering science and an evolutionary view of religion without losing faith. I have attempted to demonstrate that God's existence and influence do not conflict with science and evolutionary theory. Furthermore, developmental processes, of which evolution is one, are core concepts in the Bahá'í Faith. Humanity evolves, our spirits evolve, and society and religion evolve. We thus need not be afraid that teaching children about evolution will lead them astray or destroy their faith. It is also no longer necessary for the devout to fear science or rational argument. The rational mind, of which science is a fruit, is 'God's greatest gift to man'.[41] But pure rationality (personified in technology), devoid of the unifying and humane themes of religion, will lead us to destruction. Religion, devoid of rationality, leads us inevitably to superstition and bigotry. With the two wings of science and religion in harmony, humanity can fly to far greater heights. Let it be so.

5

Knowledge and Faith

We are all born without knowledge or religious beliefs. During our lives we acquire knowledge which may lead us to acquire certain religious convictions. Many people somehow reach a certitude in their beliefs, presumably based on knowledge that they have acquired. The role of knowledge in achieving certitude is not entirely straightforward, however. In particular, there is a tendency to associate certainty of faith with certainty of knowledge. This leads to an absolutism of conviction known as fanaticism. Such attitudes lead to bigotry, religious oppression and the persecution of minorities, as has happened to the Bahá'ís in Iran. Thus the ability to distinguish what we know from what we believe and the question of how we acquire knowledge are serious issues. Understanding these issues helps us achieve faith without fanaticism.

The issue of knowledge versus faith has become especially acute in recent years owing to widespread rejection of religious authorities in preference to individual interpretation. The Reformation was caused by a rejection of the absolute authority of the Catholic Church owing to certain excesses on its part, but it set in motion a cascading societal rejection of all authority, especially in the United States today, where stubborn individualism is a deeply-rooted part of the national character. The result has been a fragmentation of the church as an institution in that country and an emphasis on the single individual as a sufficient spiritual unit. It is believed by millions that all they need is themselves and their Bible and that God speaks to them directly. From this point of view a church is only a convenient place for like-minded people to come together, a place that has a choir and a basketball team for the youth. The concepts of discipline and obedience are rejected in favour of individual interpretation. Many televangelists are completely free of any institutional restraint and cannot be disciplined even for serious crimes. Another example of this same frame of mind may be seen in the wandering holy men of India. The result of the breaking of the restraining influence of institutional discipline is that any self-proclaimed preacher or guru can spread any kind of teaching whatsoever. And yet religion should be for the guidance and advancement of peoples and societies, not for the enrichment of televangelists or nut cases. Religion should be a reliable guide to life, a lighthouse, a safe haven, not a fashion show subject to every passing fad.

Fundamental to this dilemma is a widespread misunderstanding of the nature of knowledge. It has become common to confuse knowledge with familiarity. For example, we think that we know someone because we are familiar with him, recognize his face, and have an emotional attachment to him. In the same way people claim to know God and to have a personal relationship with His Son. Given this, in the absence of any framework of institutional obedience, it is a simple step to the presumption that God speaks to one directly. Thus the televangelist who was caught with a prostitute said that he would not step down from his ministry because 'God told him' not to. There are few bounds on what is permitted when each individual is certain that he is spoken to directly. In Islamic countries we see this same phenomenon in the common belief that every event that happens is a direct sign from God to the person concerned. For example, if the alarm clock fails to go off, it may be taken as a sign that one was not 'meant' to be on time for work, when in fact the failure of the alarm was because no one set it.* While it is of course true that people have religious and mystical experiences, even very profound and miraculous ones, it is very dangerous to confuse the experience of the numinous with an understanding of it or direct knowledge of God's Will. This is not to say that God does not answer prayers or provide guidance, but He does not sit in our living room and chat with us. Thus if the clear law laid down by God via His Prophets forbids adultery, a personal 'revelation'

*This outlook is based upon a branch of Islamic theology which became dominant in the ninth and tenth centuries. This Ash'ari theology holds that there is no such thing as causality, that every movement or event is directly caused by God's will and not by a prior event. This view is based on the Qur'ánic verse that no leaf falls from a tree without God's knowledge.

that one is excepted from this law is nothing more than wishful thinking. Thus while having mystic experiences does increase our faith, our fervour, our devotion, and our certitude, it is not the same as seeing Him. Only Moses looked upon His face in the burning bush and He could not endure it. How can we claim to know Him when in truth even one's spouse or parents, indeed one's very self, is full of surprises and disappointments. How could one be surprised by someone's behaviour if one truly knows him? On a number of occasions I have spoken to people who are certain that they know God or Jesus in this direct, encompassing, intimate sort of way, and I have asked them to describe Him (either God or Jesus) to me. In every case I have been met by utter and complete silence. This is not surprising to a Bahá'í because Bahá'ís claim that it is not possible to know God directly. We can no more know God directly than we can see gravity or hear electro-magnetic waves without the aid of a radio (see 'God Under the Microscope' in this book). That, in fact, is the very reason why we must turn to the Manifestations of God such as Jesus and Bahá'u'lláh, because only they can reveal God to us. This is the reason why one will never hear a Bahá'í speaker claim to have spoken to God directly or to have been told to say or do thus and so via a personal conversational revelation.

Before delving more deeply into this topic of the Bahá'í view of the limitations of human knowledge and how this impacts on our concept of religion itself, it is useful to explore this topic from the viewpoint of science. That is, in science how is it that we acquire knowledge and what type of knowledge can we obtain? Since science is more objectively testable than are statements about one's relationship to God, this may help clarify this subject.

In science we never know a thing in itself, but only properties or attributes of that thing. We do not know what mass is, only that objects have mass. We can measure mass as resistance to acceleration, but only 'know' mass in this context of how to measure it. We can control electricity and use it every day but we do not 'know' it. The sense of knowing things has to do with a feeling of familiarity. In the quantum theory world of atoms and particles this sense of familiarity breaks down and we are forced to face the fact that all we really know about things in this domain are their attributes and the rules governing their behaviour. It is possible to specify these rules and attributes for elementary particles, but the particles themselves do not lend themselves to this feeling of familiar knowing because the rules and properties that govern their behaviours do not resemble those at our scale of everyday living. It is not possible to 'know' what it is like inside a black hole, for example, because there is not a single frame of reference we can relate to it. How can we grasp quantum tunnelling, space-time singularities, massless particles and curved space? We may define their formal properties, equations and behaviours, but it is nonsense to say that we know them. The feeling of knowing is just as deceptive in the case of more ordinary situations, but we are only rarely made aware of it. We catch a glimpse of the true limits of our knowledge when unusual circumstances alter our perception slightly so that we are taken out of our usual sense of familiarity. A long hike in the woods may open up our senses to an awareness of the vibrancy and complexity of life that we had been missing. Falling in love may change our perception so that every moment becomes a poem. The odd or hostile behaviour of a loved one may cause us to question whether we ever really knew him or her. These are unfamiliar experiences of the familiar.

Thus in science the emphasis is on the observable properties and attributes of objects and forces. It was not until science shifted its focus from mysterious essences to observable properties and attributes that real scientific progress became possible. Galileo was the first major scientist to make this distinction, and by doing so he not only made the most rapid scientific progress that had been made up until his time, but broke the rusty shackles that had held science back. In the world of science defined by Aristotle which had ruled for 2,000 years, the essences of things were central to the definitions of those things. The essence of combustibility, for example, was a property called phlogiston. Salt contained the substance called solubility and metals contained the substance called mercury which allowed them to become fluid. The search for essences was, in the long run, counterproductive, because these essences were not observable. The great innovation of Galileo was to focus his investigation on those properties which could be observed, measured and quantified. He further held that experimentation should be used to uncover these laws. Using this approach he focused his investigations on a few topics which he studied from many angles, including the laws of motion and astronomy. He did not attempt to find essences but only the laws governing the observable properties of things.

We see a similar evolution of approach in the Bahá'í revelation. In contrast to the endless theological speculation on the nature of God that has clogged the libraries of the world with mountains of paper, the Bahá'í focus is on the observable properties of the divine as revealed by His Messengers. That is, we do not pretend ourselves capable of knowing what God is in Himself or in His essence, but only to attempt to grasp what are His attributes. Just as we do not really know what mass is but know how to measure it, Bahá'ís, similarly, do not seek after an impossible sense of familiarity with something beyond all familiarity but rather seek to know those attributes which we are capable of knowing. The strong desire to achieve familiarity combined with the ease with which a word that is often spoken comes to sound familiar can create the dangerous illusion that we actually know the unknowable, the unfathomable, the ineffable. We desire certainty of knowledge but the only thing available to us is certainty of faith. This scientific approach which emphasizes attributes over essences is reflected in the Bahá'í writings. As 'Abdu'l-Bahá states:

> As our knowledge of things, even of created and limited things, is knowledge of their qualities and not of their essence, how is it possible to comprehend in its essence the Divine Reality, which is unlimited? For the inner essence of anything is not compre-

hended, but only its qualities. For example, the inner essence of the sun is unknown, but is understood by its qualities, which are heat and light. The inner essence of man is unknown and not evident, but by its qualities it is characterized and known. Thus everything is known by its qualities and not by its essence.[1]

In order to achieve wisdom and avoid fanaticism, it is necessary to give up this misguided desire for familiarity and face our true limitations. Bahá'u'lláh explains why we must give this up and what the consequence is:

To every discerning and illumined heart it is evident that God, the unknowable Essence, the divine Being, is immensely exalted above every human attribute, such as corporeal existence, ascent and descent, egress and regress. Far be it from His glory that human tongue should adequately recount His praise, or that human heart comprehend His fathomless mystery. He is and hath ever been veiled in the ancient eternity of His Essence, and will remain in His Reality everlastingly hidden from the sight of men. 'No vision taketh in Him, but He taketh in all vision; He is the Subtile, the All-Perceiving.' (Qur'án 6:103) No tie of direct intercourse can possibly bind Him to His creatures. He standeth exalted beyond and above all separation and union, all proximity and remoteness. No sign can indicate His presence or His absence; inasmuch as by a word of His command all that are in Heaven and on earth have come to exist, and by His wish, which is the Primal Will itself, all have stepped out of utter nothingness into the realm of being, the world of the visible.

Gracious God! How could there be conceived any

existing relationship or possible connection between
His Word and they that are created of it? The verse:
'God would have you beware of Himself' (Qur'án
3:28) unmistakably beareth witness to the reality of
Our argument, and the words: 'God was alone; there
was none else besides Him' are a sure testimony of its
truth. All the Prophets of God and their chosen
Ones, all the divines, the sages, and the wise of every
generation, unanimously recognize their inability to
attain unto the comprehension of that Quintessence
of all truth, and confess their incapacity to grasp
Him, Who is the inmost Reality of all things.

The door of the knowledge of the Ancient of Days
being thus closed in the face of all beings, the Source
of infinite grace, according to His saying: 'His grace
hath transcended all things; My grace hath encom-
passed them all' hath caused those luminous Gems of
Holiness to appear out of the realm of the spirit, in
the noble form of the human temple, and be made
manifest unto all men, that they may impart unto the
world the mysteries of the unchangeable Being, and
tell of the subtleties of His imperishable Essence.[2]

Thus when we recognize our utter remoteness from
direct contact with God, we are forced to recognize
our need for the Manifestation as our guide and
refuge. Furthermore, we are told to look to the
qualities and attributes of the Manifestation. This
exactly parallels the new specific approach developed
by Galileo: focus on the observable attributes rather
than on the essences.

How is it that the divine wisdom appears in the
Prophets for us to see? What is the nature of this

connection between the physical world and the world of spirit? The following from 'Abdu'l-Bahá helps clarify this issue:

> The Divine Reality is sanctified from singleness, then how much more from plurality. The descent of that Lordly Reality into conditions and degrees would be equivalent to imperfection and contrary to perfection, and is, therefore, absolutely impossible . . .
>
> . . . the Perfect Man (the Divine Manifestation) is in the condition of a clear mirror in which the Sun of Reality becomes visible and manifest with all its qualities and perfections. So the Reality of Christ was a clear and polished mirror of the greatest purity and fineness. The Sun of Reality, the Essence of Divinity, reflected itself in this mirror and manifested its light and heat in it; but from the exaltation of its holiness, and the heaven of its sanctity, the Sun did not descend to dwell and abide in the mirror.[3]

A consequence of the impossibility of achieving absolute knowledge of the essence of things in science is that the search for understanding is never completed. If one could find the essence of a thing, nothing else would remain to be discovered. But since we can not find essences, we are forced to measure what is measurable (our 'facts' or data) and propose laws to explain these facts. No such law or fact can ever go unquestioned because new discoveries in other areas may change our understanding of it. There is no absolute certainty in science. What scientists do have, however, is faith in the *process* of science. They have a conviction that the method is valid, the goal worthy and the ends attainable. It is this same type of certitude that Bahá'ís manifest. It is a certitude based on the experience of finding answers, experiencing spiritual growth and witnessing small miracles daily. This is certitude of faith which is not to be confused with certitude of knowledge.

Just as in science where the structure of knowledge is never complete, so also in the Bahá'í Faith. The moment of accepting Bahá'u'lláh, the moment of rebirth, is indeed a divine moment that opens all the doors, but we must step through the doors and climb the steps one by one. He has given us guidance for the upward ascent in the form of *The Seven Valleys* and *The Four Valleys*, books about the search for God. He makes it clear that the spiritual life is a quest, not a place; a journey, not a condition. We observe that in a marriage those who stop trying, stop bathing, stop bringing flowers once the honeymoon is over because they have achieved their goal, soon fall into estrangement. Deep love is a process, not a thing, and only continual attention will keep it. One must continually try to get to know the other person, earn his or her love, grow as an individual, and help the other. In the same way, thinking that one has 'arrived' spiritually is the death of spirituality. It is the process of searching for the Friend that brings us closer to Him. We are never truly worthy; it is only by striving to reach Him that we become worthy. Thus it is that both deepening and prayer are enjoined upon Bahá'ís to aid their constant growth and spiritual attainment. Our approach to divine knowledge should be like that of the legendary character Majnún, searching even in the dust for his beloved. In the Bahá'í Faith the quest for knowledge and the search for God are entwined and indeed are one and the same.

6

Growth and Stability
of the Bahá'í Administrative Order

Lessons from Biology

The Bahá'í Faith is undergoing rapid worldwide growth. This growth is an organic process and as such has many features in common with the growth of other living things. There are general principles pertaining to all living systems which I propose to examine here in order to throw light on the various processes affecting Bahá'í institutions and the spread of the Cause of God.

Growth

One of the clearest generalizations throughout the living world is that large complex creatures take longer to reach maturity than small simple ones. It is not merely that time is required to reach a larger size, because small creatures such as plankton are capable of increases in total mass of a thousand-fold in a matter of weeks. Rather, large creatures require more time for the elaboration of complex structures. Building a large coherent structure requires more time and energy than building a large shapeless mass. This principle is immutable and applies equally to the Bahá'í Faith. Those of us who are Bahá'ís are sometimes frustrated by the slow growth of the Cause of God. While growth of the Cause could be much faster, some of the slowness is due to the necessity of building a large, coherent, sturdy structure that will be stable and resist perturbations. Many things could be done to speed up drastically its growth, but they would have adverse long-term consequences. For example, having ministers or priests would speed up growth because many people like to be led, but the divinely revealed administrative order of Bahá'u'lláh is participative and requires local involvement, so the dependency and passivity that result from possession of a priesthood would be detrimental in the long run. In particular, the risk of schism that arises from dependence on charismatic religious popularizers far outweighs the benefits of rapid growth that such leaders could bring. Appeals to people's fears or baser instincts (such as racial exclusivity) would also draw large crowds but would be completely contrary to the Faith's basic principles. The only sure way to achieve rapid growth is for each and every Bahá'í to play his or her small part: to live the life, participate in the administrative order, teach, pray and study the writings. There are no shortcuts consistent with the Faith's overall goals.

In order to get a better feel for the nature of the necessary trade-offs between rapid growth and permanence, let us examine the growth habits of the largest and longest-lived organisms on earth: trees. Because weeds only reach heights of a few metres at most, they do not require strong stems for support. In fact, their stems are often hollow. In contrast, trees grow much taller and must invest more of their available energy in a strong stem for future support. Thus a weed one foot tall can grow much more rapidly than a tree seedling one foot tall. But structural support is only part of the story. In order for a tree to live for hundreds of years, its trunk must withstand attacks by insects and decay year after year. In some areas periodic fires are a danger. In order to protect the trunk from fire, some species have evolved very thick bark. Protection from decay and insects is provided by growing wood that is denser than that which is strictly necessary for support. Extra lignin is added to the wood to increase its density because lignin is very resistant to decay and insects find it indigestible. Chemicals such as resins and turpenes are added to the wood as the tree ages further to increase decay resistance. All of these safeguards take energy from the tree which necessarily slows down the growth rate. Thus fast-growing weedy species such as pin cherry and willow trees are easily damaged by storms, are susceptible to pests and have a short lifespan.[1] Another noteworthy aspect of tree growth is that in long-lived species (except the most shade tolerant) it is generally the case that the tree must reach a great height in order to avoid being shaded out by other trees. Such species must therefore resist the tendency to branch out too much when young because this prevents the development of a strong central trunk. It is impossible both to grow tall and to branch into multiple trunks. Loehle,[2] for example, showed that trees which grow to great heights are resistant to influences (such as asymmetric lighting) which would deflect growth away from development of a straight central trunk.

We may draw several parallels here with the processes of growth in the Bahá'í Faith. The Cause of Bahá'u'lláh is destined to be a tall tree, to be world-embracing, not to be a shrub with many competing branches. The Covenant of Bahá'u'lláh (which establishes the succession and administrative order following His death) preserves this central trunk so that it may reach its full height. In order for the trunk to be resistant to decay and breakage, the wood must be strong. The institutions of the Bahá'í Faith provide the fibre and framework of the wood, but it is the individual cells that provide the strength and decay resistance. The process of deepening (intensive study), in particular deepening on the Covenant, provides this strength. Particular strength is provided by the participative style of Bahá'í administration because every Bahá'í must get involved and in so doing becomes further deepened and committed.

There is another growth strategy exhibited by a tree which is suggestive of lessons for Bahá'ís. The longleaf pine is a tall majestic pine found in the American southeast. It is the longest lived of the southern pines. It is found on sandy soils where fire is frequent due to drought conditions. To cope with fire, the longleaf has developed a unique evolutionary response. When a seed germinates, the seedling produces a thick bundle of needles at ground level. Instead of getting taller each year as most trees do, the seedling gets thicker around each year but stays right at ground level, producing a thicker and thicker cluster of needles. This is called the grass stage. During this stage it grows a deep taproot down to a level where it finds permanent water, often more than 15 feet deep. While in the grass stage, it is quite resistant to fire. The growing tip of the tree is close to the ground where temperatures are lowest during a fire and it is further protected by the thick cluster of green needles. When the seedling is sufficiently robust and has deep enough roots, it suddenly shoots up at the rate of three to six feet in height per year. In just a few years it is tall enough and has thick enough bark to survive most brush fires.

The Bahá'í Faith may be said to have been in the grass stage until recently: putting down deep roots while protected by the leafy green shelter of obscurity. The roots are the network of Assemblies, schools, radio stations, Houses of Worship, Auxiliary Boards, and deepened Bahá'ís supplemented by the extensive body of publications and translations of the writings of the Faith which provide the basic nutrition for its growth. The depth of this rooting provides the necessary condition for subsequent rapid growth, which we are now witnessing. The stage of emergence from obscurity, foretold by Shoghi Effendi, Guardian of the Bahá'í Faith, means that we have left the safety of the grass stage. Whereas before the fires of controversy just passed overhead, now we too become a target. Rapid growth is essential at this stage in the life of the Bahá'í community in order to pass through it safely. To falter leaves us in a very vulnerable position

We become vulnerable to attack because we are noticed but have small numbers. We become vulnerable when our credibility is questioned as the outside world begins to expect us to put Bahá'u'lláh's teachings into practice in the life of society, even though we may not be financially or administratively ready to do so.

The Bahá'í Faith has spread remarkably rapidly to all parts of the world during the past century. Again, analogies may be drawn with biological processes. There is a particular case that is instructive and I hope the reader will not mind that this example involves an agricultural weed. This weed was studied in farm fields in South Carolina in an effort to exterminate it or at least to control its spread. The weed was found to grow in numbers slowly within individual fields but to spread to distant fields as seeds riding on agricultural equipment. Upon entering a new field it would very gradually increase in that field, being apparently rare there for a long time but providing seeds to be carried to further fields. A computer model of the spatial spread of this pest led to interesting conclusions. As the weed spread in this island-hopping manner, the populations in the newly colonized fields would be very low and easy to overlook. It would go unnoticed until suddenly, after a few years, it would have occupied most fields in an entire county and overrun them. This is because each isolated population was growing exponentially but starting from very small numbers. Because the population was scattered, the numbers appeared smaller than they actually were and the true rate of growth was not evident. This type of exponential growth, based on constant dispersal to outlying areas, is exactly what we see in the progress of the Bahá'í Faith as a consequence of the plans of 'Abdu'l-Bahá and Shoghi Effendi. Thus whereas the growth of the Faith may seem slow to Bahá'ís, the methods being followed are in the long run the best for the most rapid spreading of the Faith to the whole globe. Interestingly, for this strategy to work, it is necessary that all propagules (small groups, pioneers) be capable of themselves spreading the Cause. Because all Bahá'ís are enjoined to deepen and teach and do not depend on a priesthood, this condition is fully met.

A characteristic of all growth processes is that energy is required. To examine the trees again, energy is captured from sunlight and partitioned into roots, stems and leaves. If this partitioning is not balanced, the tree will die. For example, in drier habitats the tree must put more of its captured energy into roots or it will not survive a drought. In the process of growth of the Bahá'í Faith in any one locality, this principle also applies. We may compare the leaves to teaching activities, the stem to the institutions and the roots to deepening activities. If all effort goes into teaching, this is like a tree without a trunk. There is no means for lifting the leaves up and protecting them from adversity. After a time the leaves will become starved for nutrition and will perish. A tree that consists only of a trunk and roots is like a well-organized community with an Assembly and committees but without teaching. No matter how strong the trunk such a tree cannot grow. A tree with shallow roots will blow down with the first storm or wither in the first drought. Thus the key to successful growth is a balance between the different structures that make up the organism (organization).

A further aspect of the growth process is the rhythm of growth. In most organisms, growth usually occurs in spurts rather than in a steady fashion. This is because the resources needed for growth are more available at certain times, such as spring, than at others. In order to achieve rapid growth in the spring, trees use energy stored over the winter as starches and sugars. It is very important for the tree to grow as rapidly as possible while conditions are optimal, so it draws down its energy reserves very low at this time. Because its energy reserves are low, the tree is in a delicate situation with respect to damaging agents. Heavy pruning of a tree in late spring can be very damaging, for example. Overly rapid growth can actually cause death. Some brands of herbicides work by causing the weeds to grow so fast that they use up all of their stored energy reserves and starve to death. The same danger of low energy reserves can occur during the expansion of a local Bahá'í community if growth is too rapid and uncoordinated: the energy of the individual Bahá'ís may be completely used up and inactivity can result.

Thus, overall, there is a natural rhythm of growth and a necessary balance to the components of the community for growth to be sustained. Growth must not be too rapid nor unbalanced, nor on the other hand should opportunities for growth be passed by. When conditions are right, growth can and should be rapid. The need for energy reserves to be available to attain rapid growth suggests that a community should not over-commit itself to committees and other structures so that some energy is available to put into growth when the time is right. By knowing how growth is best achieved in nature, we can similarly increase the balanced growth of the Bahá'í community.

Stability

For any growing system, we must consider not only growth but stability. A cancer has the property of growth but not of stability because it destroys the organism of which it is a part. Stability may be illustrated with some examples. A ball sitting at the bottom of a bowl is stable. If not disturbed it will tend to remain where it is. It also tends to return to its position after being disturbed because gravity pulls it back to the bottom of the bowl. This is resilience. In contrast, a rock sitting on the edge of a cliff is stable, because it does not move if not disturbed, but is not resilient because the slightest movement sends it over the cliff. This is a metastable condition. We may also speak of stability or resilience of structure or function. A rock sitting on the ground has a stable structure except over a very long time span, whereas an ice cube sitting in the sun is not stable at all and melts quickly. A more advanced type of stability is exhibited by organisms because they take energy to maintain themselves and use information from the environment (feedback) to regulate their condition. We term this homeostasis. The simplest example of a homeostatic system is a thermostat. If the temperature falls below the setpoint, the furnace comes on, while if the temperature rises above the set-point, the furnace goes off. Information about temperature is used by the thermostat to regulate the temperature in the house. Organisms use a variety of sources of information such as hunger as an indicator of a need for food and body temperature as an indicator of a need to sweat or seek shelter.

Organizations also use information to regulate their behaviour so as to maintain themselves. For example, the Roman Empire maintained itself for about a thousand years despite all kinds of disturbances and problems. The ability of an organization to respond to changes in conditions and to maintain itself depends on what internal structures and mechanisms of response it has. For example, the downfall of dictators often results from their total isolation from bad news, since such news may be seen by them as criticism and opposition. Failure to respond to bad news leads to worsening of conditions in the society or to disastrous military encounters. Hitler's behaviour towards the end of the Second World War is an excellent example of this. He refused to admit or acknowledge the bad news from the Russian front and insisted that victory was near during the Battle of the Bulge in the West, when in fact his army was almost out of fuel and devastated in numbers.

There is a tendency for people to create very rigid social structures rather than adaptable ones because this increases the feeling of security of the leaders of the organizations. Rigid social structures have the appearance of strength but do not have flexibility. We may compare them to a tall office building. In building earthquake resistance into a tall building, the initial concept was just to make everything stronger and more rigid. It was soon found, however, that designing flexibility into the building so that it sways and vibrates in response to an earthquake led to better earthquake resistance. Extremely rigid structures tolerate small quakes but when a larger one hits they may go completely to pieces. Organizations behave very similarly. Very rigid structures cannot adapt to changing conditions and will literally go to pieces under severe stress, forming many splinter groups. One of the characteristics of a rigid structure is an extreme emphasis on hierarchies and on ritual. The emphasis in such organizations is on obedience rather than on participation, on subservience rather than unity.

The administrative structures in the Bahá'í Faith are extraordinarily well-designed for flexibility and adaptability. The electoral process for Local Spiritual Assemblies encourages participation rather than mere subservience. Adaptability is ensured by the Assembly's ability to create ad hoc committees at will and by the community's ability to elect different individuals if conditions change. No individuals have lifetime or career leadership positions. The development of rigid hierarchies is prevented by the lack of a central individual of authority such as a priest. Authority is dispersed throughout the community. This same property of dispersed authority helps prevent fragmentation of the Faith. The institutions of the learned (the Auxiliary Boards) are protected from becoming too rigid in structure by having limited terms of service rather than lifelong appointments and by the separation of the institution of the rulers from that of the learned. That is, those appointed to the institution of the learned because of their learning and ability to inspire are not given any administrative responsibilities or financial authority. The lack of emphasis on ritual means that participation rather than blind obedience is encouraged. This system is adaptable to changing conditions because of the dual nature of the administrative structure. Spiritual guidance comes down from the Universal House of Justice via the institution of the learned, but practical implementation of goals occurs at the local level of administration where the people know better how to adapt the goals to their local conditions, resources and level of development. Overall, the Bahá'í administrative order is remarkably flexible, adaptable and homeostatic.

A key aspect of homeostatic systems is the manner in which homeostasis is maintained. A system that is homeostatic is always adjusting itself to maintain the desired state. Animals must constantly adjust food intake to meet their needs and balance the time they spend in various activities. An acrobat on a high wire similarly is constantly adjusting his balance. The effectiveness of homeostasis depends on the way information is used and on how homeostasis is maintained. For example, an inexperienced person walking a high wire cannot tell that he is leaning to one side until the tilt is extreme, at which point he must quickly shift his weight to the other side. This may lead to overshoot, the wild waving of arms and a fall. The information feedback concerning position is not finely tuned and the response is not well controlled, causing oscillations. We may examine local Bahá'í administration in this context of homeostatic control.

Since local Bahá'í communities are governed in a participative manner, many members of the community are involved in the homeostatic process. Efforts to restore balance are often initiated by the perception of 'problems' such as inactivity, burnout or disharmony. Because Bahá'ís are very involved and very concerned about unity, it is disturbing for them to encounter 'problems'. To some it is even disillusioning. It is important to realize, however, that in a homeostatic system in a changing environment 'problems' will always exist because the equilibrium can never be maintained for long. As soon as the Local Spiritual Assembly is trained and functioning well, someone on it may move away. New situations and opportunities constantly arise. It is helpful to realize that feedback and change are essential parts of a self-regulating system. This shifts our focus so that we can see 'problems' as information and can put our energy into the feedback and adaptive mechanisms of the organization, rather than becoming overwrought because 'problems' exist. Remembering the acrobat, it is crucial to get information quickly so that it can be responded to before an imbalance becomes too great.

An important means for achieving this goal is unity of action. The Bahá'í teachings enjoin Bahá'ís and their communities to be united in obedience to decisions of the Spiritual Assembly. This is not a mindless obedience, but rather creates clear feedback on decisions and actions so that the next decisions made will be better. Let us say that the community decides to have a picnic at a certain park. Two people are convinced that a different park would be better. If these two people fail to co-operate, they can sabotage the picnic. The fact that the picnic fails, however, does nothing to prove whether one park is better or not, because the information is muddied by the noise of disunity covering the signal of true results. If everyone participates and the picnic is still not much fun, then it is clear that the cause is the site and not disunity. A united response enables clear, unambiguous feed-back on the actions taken. This both helps maintain balance and promotes institutional learning.

The second component of achieving a successful homeostatic system is the nature of the response mechanism. Inappropriate response can cause over-shoot or under-response. The first criterion for suc-cessful response is that the administrative body be receptive to information. It is characteristic of rigid hierarchical systems that they keep information out. Only those with privilege have access to the upper hierarchy. Since politicians have precisely this problem but must get reelected, they have come to depend on opinion polls to obtain information from outside their organization.

The Bahá'í administrative structure is particularly open to the influx of information. Information on the state of the world and of the Bahá'í community at large is passed down to Local Assemblies by the Auxiliary Boards and the higher administrative bodies. The Local Assembly meets with the whole community at the feast, every 19 days, at which time community suggestions and problems are passed on to the Assembly. This is very different from most church structures.

A destabilizing factor in any homeostatic system is the presence of lags. If one does not balance the chequebook for many months, a major imbalance can result. The fact that many Local Spiritual Assemblies meet only every few weeks or once a month means that lags between problem origination and problem solution can result, leading both to growth of problems and missed opportunities. The recognition of this tendency has already led to changes in Bahá'í procedure. For example, it is cumbersome for an Assembly to work directly with the media; therefore, most Assemblies have delegated public information officers who can respond quickly to media opportunities. The new use of teaching institutes is another example. It was clear that when all teaching activities were organized by the Assembly the delays induced tended to dampen enthusiasm. Teaching institutes empower individuals and groups to initiate teaching activities without this type of delay. This has been a very successful programme.

A third critical factor is that homeostatic responses must be flexible. There is a tendency for organizations to establish rigid habits because particular methods worked in the past and are therefore continued. To maintain an effective homeostatic mechanism it is essential that the organization be able freely to consider all options. It must be willing to reverse its own previous decisions if appropriate. The Bahá'í consultative process encourages this flexibility. This is because ideas or plans belong to the group and not to individuals; thus if the plan is changed no individual loses face. In addition, because everyone's ideas are solicited, a wider spectrum of ideas is available for consideration.

The final criterion is adaptive response. An adaptive response is characterized by the anticipation of problems and patterns to create a more sophisticated response. For example, the acrobat knows by habit that after correcting his balance to the left he will probably have to make a further minor adjustment back to the right, and thus begins to prepare the left leg for this in advance. Trees leaf out well in advance of optimal weather in spring so as to be fully ready when it arrives. An adaptive administrative response anticipates the seasonal and emotional ups and downs of the community, planning appropriately.

These several criteria, which apply to any adaptive system, can help us understand Bahá'í administration as an organic process. In this context most problems are really just sources of information for adjusting course. Understanding the feedback/response process can help us fine tune this process and avoid destructive extremes such as inactivity and burnout.

In conclusion, we can see that several general principles of growth and stability apply to Bahá'í administrative structures just as they do to any system. Growth must be harmonized in its parts in order for rapid growth to be achievable. Guidance given to Bahá'í communities which emphasizes a balance between teaching, administration and consolidation properly harmonizes these elements.

Resilience and stability are also key system properties specifically provided for in the Baha'ı administrative structure. Overall, the Baha'ı administrative structure is one of remarkable flexibility, adaptiveness and growth capacity.

7

Entropy and the Integrity
of the Sacred Texts

One of the avowed reasons for the coming of
Bahá'u'lláh is to renew God's Word among men. And
yet, why should God's Word need to be renewed? If
it is sacred, should it not be unchanging? We may
begin to answer this question by noting that every
material thing is subject to decay. In the case of
the holy writings, it is not necessarily the written
word itself which suffers decomposition or decay but
the language of which it is composed. Language
inexorably suffers from changes in word meaning,
spelling and grammar. Events and stories are inevitably culture-bound, so that as culture changes
over time (e.g. from rural to urban) the interpretation of events changes even if word meanings *per se*
have not changed. Thus the message contained in
written text gradually suffers decay over time as the
reader becomes progressively unable to interpret it.
English from Chaucer's time, for example, is very
difficult for modern readers to understand and
Beowolf in the original is, for the layperson, completely unreadable. Thus there is reason to suspect
that holy texts might also suffer from corruption of

meaning and interpretability over time and need renewal. In fact, this is one of the reasons that Bahá'u'lláh gives for religion needing periodic renewal: that the people have lost and corrupted the original Word of God.

A scientific perspective throws a new light on this topic. One useful conceptual framework, derived from thermodynamics, is information theory, and particularly the information-theoretic implications of entropy. Entropy is a principle of physics which posits that disorganized states are more likely to exist than are organized states and that energy must be expended to move from a disorganized to an organized state. Anyone with small children knows the vanishingly small probability that the result of their play will be a neat and well-organized house. In a closed system complete disorder is the ultimate, most likely state. Only with a constant input of energy can a complex system be maintained. Our bodies require food (energy) constantly, for example, to maintain themselves. The same is true of any complex structure.

All messages must be encoded in some physical form, whether in letters, magnetic media, pictures or sound. Any such physical representation of an idea is subject to errors at the stages of encoding, transmission and decoding. Energy is required for all of these processes and thereby they become subject to entropy. Preservation over time also requires continued input of energy. Even assuming that the message itself is flawlessly encoded (i.e. is divinely-inspired and perfectly transcribed), there are three main mechanisms of message degradation: 1) the written document itself (e.g. over time documents tend to fade, get torn or become lost); 2) the transmission to a receptor (e.g. misperception of a word due to fatigue or poor lighting); and 3) the decoding of the message (e.g. the very common problem of someone misunderstanding what they read, especially if it is on an unfamiliar topic).

Let us consider the genetic code, DNA. DNA consists of long chains of molecules, called bases. There are a limited number of combinations of these bases, each of which codes for an amino acid. The order of the genetic code determines the order in which amino acids are assembled into proteins, which in turn regulate the mechanisms of the body. Disorder enters the picture in the form of mutations. The forces buffeting a DNA chain are relatively strong compared to the strength of the chemical bonds which bind it together. For example, ionizing radiation may break the bonds in a DNA molecule, causing a mutation which is likely to change the structure of the protein for which that piece of DNA is the code or even to create nonsense at that spot so that no protein can be coded. Mistakes also occur during cell replication. Over time, mistakes tend to build up, degrading the information content of the DNA and causing abnormalities. Natural selection tends to prune out those individuals with harmful mutations because they cannot compete. Mutations are also, however, the means by which new, beneficial traits enter the arena so that evolution can proceed.

We may draw a very close parallel between the

effect of entropic forces on DNA and on written documents. Assume for a moment that we have a perfectly precise document which is preserved unchanged over time. The words of which this document is composed do, however, change over time in the meanings given to them by any reader. This process of mutation of word meaning and spelling is inevitable. As culture changes and progresses, language also changes. Language and culture are intimately and inextricably bound together and it is inevitable that culture changes over time. Therefore language also changes. In addition, random changes in word usage and meaning occur. For example, in the biblical parable of the ten talents, a talent is a Roman coin but its common usage has become that of a skill. In very ancient texts this problem is rampant. There are hundreds of words in the Bible, for example, whose original meanings differ from current usage. Even significant words such as 'domesday' have meanings that have drastically altered over time. 'Domesday' in the King James Bible refers to the judgement day. It is derived from the Old English 'dom' meaning 'law' or 'judgement'. 'Domesday' in popular understanding, however, has come to be synonymous with doom or destruction or the end of everything. In the Old Testament the names of many plants and animals are given, but without any descriptions. After the passage of two to three thousand years we are no longer able to ascertain to what creatures these words refer. Many cities and places referred to in the Bible are gone or cannot be located. To compound the problem, ancient Aramaic, the language spoken by Jesus, is a dead language, as are biblical Greek and Hebrew.

Even if we accept that a holy text, as God's Word, is under His protection, we must recognize that the language people use to understand it is constantly changing. Just as an organism whose DNA never mutated would never progress and would even be unable to keep up with changes in its environment over the millenia, so also must language change for a society to grow and adapt to new circumstances. The consequence of this is that the meaning of the holy texts becomes progressively obscure over the centuries. Since God would not allow His Word to become obliterated, we must conclude that there is some means by which He overcomes this dilemma. The solution, of course, is that He periodically sends a Messenger to renew His message. Thus we see that the concept that God's Word as embodied in His book (for example, the Bible or Qur'án) is unchanging and fixed is in direct conflict with the natural process He has ordained for the progress of civilization: the evolution and development of language as a vehicle for culture. If language is fixed in stone, culture cannot progress; but if language changes, then we progressively lose touch with the written Word of God. Attempts by ordinary people to purify or renew God's Word have only led to sectarian splintering and actual worsening of the effects of entropy via theological disputations which distort word meaning and fallacious but attractive arguments which cause conceptual confusion. There is no alternative but periodic renewal of the pure divine message and this can only be achieved by a divine Messenger. In between episodes of renewal, we might expect there to be some mechanism whereby as much meaning as possible is preserved. One clear mechanism of this type is the use of parables.

Message Transmission and Parables

When any message is transmitted by any medium, noise degrades the signal to some extent, again due to entropy. This is true of voice, radio, telephone or hand signals. We also note that when there is noise of this type, the severity of the problem increases non-linearly with the number of bits of information lost. A few missing letters in a facsimile transmission are easily filled in, but when five to ten per cent of the letters are missing, the entire meaning may be lost. In the case of the words of the Prophets, their message is being communicated down the centuries rather than down a wire, but noise (changes in word meaning, discussed above) nevertheless degrades the signal. Considering again a fax transmission, we note that a high contrast image composed of bold, straight lines and without fine detail will transmit most reliably. The effectiveness of parables may be traced to an analogous mechanism. On the surface, parables are a little bit obscure because they do not come right out and state their meaning; however, they are thereby able to communicate rather abstract concepts.

. . . the human spirit is an intellectual, not sensible reality. In explaining these intellectual realities, one is obliged to express them by sensible figures, because in exterior existence there is nothing that is not material . . . So the symbol of knowledge is light, and of ignorance darkness; but reflect, is knowledge sensible light, or ignorance sensible darkness? No, they are merely symbols.[1]

Parables also have the very desirable property of being quite robust to translation and to changes in word meaning over time. It is far easier to translate the story of the prodigal son, for example, than an abstract theological treatise on the nature of the soul. Words such as son, father, orchard and money refer to concrete objects and tend to have few meanings. A message composed of such words and describing a sequence of events in the form of a story will remain intact and interpretable far longer than one composed of such words as spirit, duty, honour and sin, which typically have many, context-dependent and shifting meanings.

Although parables are robust in this sense, they are also ambiguous and lack precision. This makes many people uncomfortable. They want to be told exactly what to do and what to believe in order to be saved. This leads to an insistence on literal interpretation. Yet not even the most literal-minded believe that parables can be interpreted literally. Thus we are left with the mystery that parts of the Bible appear to be deliberately ambiguous to serve God's purpose that the meaning not be lost over time. Yet to many people the fact that it is God's Word means that it should be instantly understandable. This brings us back to the three components of communication – the message itself, its transmission and its decoding – and the means by which noise or error *entropy* may interfere with the message. Human decoding of messages is far from precise. Even the decoding of clear directions to some location often leads to one getting lost – how much more so for complex text! Human understanding is by definition limited, and this limitation is not magically waived merely because we are reading a religious work. As Bahá'u'lláh reminds us:

> Immeasurably exalted is He above the strivings of human mind to grasp His Essence, or of human tongue to describe His mystery.[2]

Furthermore, even when a message is perfectly clear, there is a human tendency to distort the message to conform to our own preconceptions or wishes. The implication is that we can never be absolutely certain of our own interpretation of holy writings. And yet we are obliged to try to understand them. Is this some cruel trick? Not at all. The requirements for reading holy texts are humility and a pure heart: humility to remember our limited capacity and our tendency to err, and a pure heart to open the doors of meaning. Christ frequently said, 'He who has an ear, let him hear', indicating the need to read very carefully and with a pure heart. In this sense, parables are like an encrypted message, where the 'key' to understanding is a prayerful approach. Bahá'u'lláh tells us:

> When a true seeker determineth to take the step of search in the path leading unto the knowledge of the Ancient of Days, he must, before all else, cleanse his

heart, which is the seat of the revelation of the inner
mysteries of God, from the obscuring dust of all
acquired knowledge, and the allusions of the em-
bodiments of satanic fancy. He must purge his
breast, which is the sanctuary of the abiding love of
the Beloved, of every defilement, and sanctify his
soul from all that pertaineth to water and clay, from
all shadowy and ephemeral attachments. He must so
cleanse his heart that no remnant of either love or
hate may linger therein, lest that love blindly incline
him to error, or that hate repel him away from the
truth.[3]

The holy books are not cookbooks or textbooks.
They are on a different plane and must be
approached with prayer and studied over and over
for their inner meanings. Thus the meanings are
accessible, but only to the sincere.

Safeguards of Meaning in the Bahá'í Sacred Writings

If it is true that the Bahá'í Faith is destined to be a
universal revelation, with an influence extending
thousands of years into the future, then we might
expect that safeguards would be present to preserve
meaning as much as possible from the entropic
effects of time and change. In fact, we observe
multiple layers of protection, many of them unique
in religious history.

One of the first and most striking of the protec-
tions in the Bahá'í revelation is that the originals of
the vast majority of the sacred texts are preserved in
the archives at the Bahá'í World Centre. Tablets of

Bahá'u'lláh are preserved by the hundreds in the handwriting of His secretaries and with His seal affixed. Never before in religious history have the words of the Prophet been recorded in writing during His lifetime and preserved in the original. Perhaps most striking is that many of the preserved Tablets are in His own hand, especially key ones such as His Will and Testament. A unique aspect of Bahá'u'lláh's handwriting is that it exhibits a tremor owing to His poisoning at the hands of his half-brother Mírzá Yahyá in Adrianople. A tremor of this type makes forgery of His penmanship almost impossible. It is like a message that has been encrypted with a secret key. Thus complete certainty as to the authenticity of these documents has been guaranteed.

We noted above that parables are robust to changes in language over time and to translation. The words 'father' and 'orchard' can be translated unambiguously into almost any language, whereas the word 'soul' cannot. We observe in the Bahá'í writings many parables and stories used to illustrate various points. These parables and stories are quite robust to translation and transcend barriers of literacy, but are of necessity somewhat ambiguous. To counter this difficulty, there also exist precise discussions of various topics, as in *The Book of Certitude* and *Some Answered Questions*. This combination of robustness and precision forms a valuable check and balance on interpretation of meaning.

We also note that in the Bahá'í dispensation parables are manifested in the form of historical events. The entire early period of Bábí and Bahá'í history referred to by the Guardian as the 'Heroic

Age' in a very real sense consists of a flood of flesh and blood parables. We may consider, for example, the parable of the prison, repeated as a theme throughout the major events of the Bahá'í revelation. This parable is unique in the annals of the world's religions and its ubiquity in Bahá'í history indicates its central significance. Time and again, for example, the Báb was moved because His gaolers became His devoted followers who would throw open the prison doors and allow Him to have visitors. It was in the dark dungeon of the Síyáh-Chál in Tehran that Bahá'u'lláh, while threatened with death at any moment, nevertheless spurred His fellow prisoners to such devotion that they chanted heroically throughout the nights until their cries reached the ears of the Shah.

We were all huddled together in one cell, our feet in stocks, and around our necks fastened the most galling of chains. The air we breathed was laden with the foulest impurities, while the floor on which we sat was covered with filth and infested with vermin. No ray of light was allowed to penetrate that pestilential dungeon or to warm its icy coldness. We were placed in two rows, each facing the other. We had taught them to repeat certain verses which, every night, they chanted with extreme fervour. 'God is sufficient unto me; He verily is the All-Sufficing!' one row would intone, while the other would reply: 'In Him let the trusting trust.' The chorus of these gladsome voices would continue until the early hours of the morning.[4]

It was in this same foul pit that Bahá'u'lláh received the call to prophethood.

While engulfed in tribulations I heard a most wondrous, a most sweet voice, calling above My head.
Turning My face, I beheld a Maiden – the embodiment of the remembrance of the name of My Lord –
suspended in the air before Me. So rejoiced was she
in her very soul that her countenance shone with
the ornament of the good-pleasure of God, and
her cheeks glowed with the brightness of the All-
Merciful. Betwixt earth and heaven she was raising a
call which captivated the hearts and minds of men.
She was imparting to both My inward and outer
being tidings which rejoiced My soul, and the souls of
God's honoured servants. Pointing with her finger
unto My head, she addressed all who are in heaven
and all who are on earth, saying: 'By God! This is the
Best-Beloved of the worlds, and yet ye comprehend
not. This is the Beauty of God amongst you, and the
power of His sovereignty within you, could ye but
understand. This is the Mystery of God and His
Treasure, the Cause of God and His glory unto all
who are in the kingdoms of Revelation and of
creation, if ye be of them that perceive.'[5]

Bahá'u'lláh prospered in spite of imprisonment and
was repeatedly banished from place to place by His
adversaries. Whereas Bahá'u'lláh arrived in Baghdad
a prisoner and exile, upon His second banishment
ten years later a multitude came to see Him off with
a tumultuous display of bereavement.

As a prisoner in Adrianpole, He began to address
the rulers of the world, lay the foundations for a new
world order, and pour forth profound, moving and
beautiful prayers and other writings. He later arrived
in 'Akká, the prison-city of Ottoman Turkey, in
complete ignominy, being confined with His fol-

lowers to two rooms in the prison barracks; but He ended His life not only living in the relative luxury and freedom of the mansion of Bahjí, but being accorded, upon His death, a degree of sympathy and grief that few kings receive.

'. . . a multitude of the inhabitants of 'Akká and of the neighbouring villages, that had thronged the fields surrounding the Mansion, could be seen weeping, beating upon their heads, and crying aloud their grief'.

For a full week a vast number of mourners, rich and poor alike, tarried to grieve with the bereaved family, partaking day and night of the food that was lavishly dispensed by its members. Notables, among whom were numbered Shí'ahs, Sunnís, Christians, Jews and Druzes, as well as poets, 'ulamás and government officials, all joined in lamenting the loss, and in magnifying the virtues and greatness of Bahá'u'lláh . . .[6]

We may briefly summarize some of the meanings inherent in this running parable. First, it is a parable of God's sovereignty and the powerlessness of the forces of this world to stop God's plan. No matter how many times the Báb and Bahá'u'lláh were exiled and imprisoned, the flood of holy writings and guidance for humankind was never stilled, nor their spirits bowed. Second, it is a parable of the transforming power of the Will of God: the transformation of a prison into God's throne, and absolute abasement into glory, making the blackest dungeon the scene of the moment of revelation. Third, when we view the prison as symbolic of the prison of self, then the parable of the prison becomes a parable of hope for each trapped soul. We are all trapped in the prison of self, the prison of desires, the prison of frailty and lack of will. This repeated parable reminds us that nothing is impossible in God's path and that no prison is binding. If Jesus' martyrdom on the cross represents the ultimate love of self-sacrifice and reminds us of God's infinite love for us, then the theme of the prison parable represents the ultimate hope of God's infinite grace, capable of freeing captive humanity from both outward and inner oppression.

We may note another recurring theme in the Heroic Age: the parable of the search. In *The Seven Valleys* and *The Four Valleys*, Bahá'u'lláh wrote of the spiritual quest metaphorically as a physical journey.

> The stages that mark the wayfarer's journey from the abode of dust to the heavenly homeland are said to be seven. Some have called these Seven Valleys, and others, Seven Cities. And they say that until the wayfarer taketh leave of self, and traverseth these stages, he shall never reach to the ocean of nearness and union, nor drink of the peerless wine. The first is THE VALLEY OF SEARCH. The steed of this valley is patience; without patience the wayfarer on this journey will reach nowhere and attain no goal. Nor should he ever be downhearted; if he strive for a hundred thousand years and yet fail to behold the beauty of the Friend, he should not falter.[7]

He goes on to elucidate the stages of the spiritual quest in captivating allegory. This spiritual quest was clothed in flesh during the Bahá'í dispensation. In the years leading up to the declaration of the Báb,

we witness the actual journeys of search of <u>Shaykh</u>
Aḥmad and Siyyid Káẓim, who were searching for
the promised one of Islam, culminating in the quest
of Mullá Ḥusayn who found the Báb and became His
<u>first disciple</u>. Others had dreams and visions and
set out upon a spiritual quest which led them to
the Báb and Bahá'u'lláh. Over the many years of
Bahá'u'lláh's exiles, hundreds made the arduous
journey to see Him, first in Baghdad and finally in
'Akká, most returning home completely trans-
formed. By making that physical journey they also
made an inner journey of immense proportions. The
outward symbol of the journey communicates an
inner reality that is difficult to convey in abstract
terms.

We may note other living parables such as the
parable of the <u>sacrifice</u> as illustrated by the thousands of <u>Persian martyrs</u>, and the parable of the
<u>Covenant,</u> in which the true meaning and power of
Bahá'u'lláh's Covenant was illustrated via the
actions and ultimate downfall of those among His
followers who arose to oppose it.

Thus many of the most profound truths and
lessons revealed by Bahá'u'lláh are not only
explained but are <u>clothed in flesh and blood</u> and are
acted out in grand display. If we cannot grasp the
theology, we need only listen to the parables as lived
by the heroes and villains of this great drama to feel
deeply touched and profoundly enlightened. When
parables are contained in history it is perhaps easy to
fail to see them, but when we do their power and
profundity is amplified many times because we are
reading a true story.

From the point of view of the reader who must decode the written word and grasp its meaning, we note that in addition to the parables and precise theological treatises mentioned above, the Bahá'í writings also contain mystic tracts such as *The Seven Valleys* and *The Four Valleys*, prayers, practical expositions of various topics, and laws and exhortations. These writings differ in the manner in which one learns from them. The beauty of this variety of modes of exposition is that there is some mode that best matches the orientation and decoding skill of most every reader. Some people most easily grasp a truth in the form of a prayer, whereas others require precise answers to certain questions. Furthermore, certain truths are more easily expressed in one mode than in others. We may only truly grasp the mystery of sacrifice and glimpse the fire of the love of God when we see the eyes of the martyrs in Iran as described in *Nabíl's Narrative (The Dawn-breakers)*. It is doubtful whether the process of searching for God could be expressed in logical terms as effectively as it is in the allegories of *The Seven Valleys* and *The Four Valleys*. Thus the variety of modes of expression in the Bahá'í writings helps to overcome the limitations of decoding ability inherent in the human condition.

An important method for preserving meaning in the face of noise is repetition. If we have several copies of a picture or text, each of which has a portion blurred or missing, we can reconstruct a complete image. Astronomers use this technique to sharpen blurred images of distant objects. In the context here, it is not the message itself that is blurred but our ability to grasp its meaning correctly. For any given passage, there is a high probability that we will not quite understand it. If, however, the same idea is repeated several times, each time expressed slightly differently, then it becomes more unlikely that we will misunderstand it. In this situation, only the correct understanding will be consistent with the several different expressions of the idea. Due to the sheer volume of the Bahá'í writings, we find that there is plenty of room for repetition. We also note that 'Abdu'l-Bahá used repetition in most of His talks and writings, repeating the same idea several times in varied forms within a single presentation. Repetition also plays a role in the admonition that Bahá'ís should study the sacred writings daily. By doing so we increase the chance, by repetition, that we will eventually grasp the truths contained therein.

It was shown above that changes in language are a major problem for preserving the integrity of holy writings. A unique feature of the Bahá'í revelation is that authenticated original texts exist in Persian, Arabic and English. This results in tremendous resilience in the face of changes in language. Consider that if a word changes in meaning in one language, it is extremely unlikely that the same word will change to the same new meaning at the same time in both of the other languages. In fact, the chance of this is vanishingly small. The ability to compare word usage in three languages provides a powerful protection against loss of interpretability and may be compared to a parity check in data communications.

One might ask why past revelations did not make use of these methods (other than parable) for preserving meaning over time against the forces of entropy. There are several reasons for this. First, much of the message in the New Testament was initially remembered and only later written down. Of necessity human memory cannot contain as much detail as volumes of written text. Even if it had been possible to write down more at the time, during long centuries of semi-literacy the church was barely able to preserve and successfully translate the amount of writings that did exist. Finally, there was a good reason more detail and precision was not given at the time of Christ. He said to His disciples that there were many things He had to tell them but that they could not bear to hear them then. To have given sufficient detail to ensure that exact meanings could be preserved over time would have required that He say more than the people could grasp, which would have created a barrier preventing people from accepting Him. Rather, He focused on the robust but less precise mode of the parable.

In conclusion we note that by applying scientific concepts such as entropy, message transmission, and parity checking we can achieve insights about the nature of the holy texts as communication vehicles, and about the limitations imposed upon them in this capacity. From this perspective we can understand the importance of parables as a message type in a new light and, looking for parables in the Bahá'í dispensation, see that many of the parables in this day are living ones.

8

Probability and Prophecy

One of the proofs of the divine origin of the Prophets throughout the ages has been the fulfilment of prophecy. Jesus referred His listeners to the prophecies of Moses and Daniel, among others. The story of the three wise men is performed every Christmas in memory of the miracle of a Zoroastrian prophecy acted upon and fulfilled. Yet the prophecies Jesus fulfilled were not so obvious that, solely by their fulfilment, people were converted *en masse*. Rather, the Jews railed against Him because they saw these prophecies as not being fulfilled.

Bahá'u'lláh names prophetic fulfilment among the proofs of the divine origin of His mission. He gives the person of the Prophet as the greatest proof, followed by His words and then by the fruits of His teachings. The fulfilment of prophecy is also given great significance. Without a promise in earlier holy books that a new Prophet would come, there would be no reason for people to change their faith, because doing so would mean denial of all they previously professed. A promise that a new Messenger will come is meaningless without some signs whereby the new Messenger may be recognized. These signs

are the prophecies, promises and visions of the seers
and sages of the past.

The Báb and Bahá'u'lláh have a definite historical
role of fulfilment of the promises and prophecies of
the past. In fact, their role is unique in fulfilling the
promises and prophecies of all the major religions of
the past. Evaluating this claim is difficult, however.
Many prophecies refer to spiritual conditions rather
than material events and can never be fulfilled in a
literal sense. We must first call to mind the essentially symbolic nature of much religious language. As
'Abdu'l-Bahá explains:

> . . . to explain them you are obliged to have recourse
> to sensible figures because in the exterior world there
> is nothing that is not sensible.
>
> So the symbol of knowledge is light, and of
> ignorance darkness; but reflect, is knowledge
> sensible light, or ignorance sensible darkness? No,
> they are merely symbols. These are only intellectual
> states, but when you desire to express them
> outwardly, you call knowledge light, and ignorance
> darkness . . .
>
> Then it is evident that the dove which descended
> upon Christ was not a material dove, but it was a
> spiritual state, which, that it might be comprehen-
> sible, was expressed by a sensible figure. Thus in the
> Old Testament it is said that God appeared as a pillar
> of fire; this does not signify the material form; it is an
> intellectual reality which is expressed by a sensible
> image.[1]

'Abdu'l-Bahá points out regarding the prophecy that
'the stars will fall from heaven', for example, that it
is impossible for the stars to literally fall upon the

earth because they are all so much larger than the earth.[2] Rather, this is a symbolic statement with the stars standing for the religious and other authorities who will fall from their positions of power upon the Return. Interpreting these prophecies requires that one's spiritual eyes and ears be open. See, for example, the chapter in this volume on 'Knowledge and Faith'.

However, even when prophecies refer to material events, places or dates, care must be taken. Before we accept the fulfilment of some prophecy as any kind of proof, it is important to be able to say how likely such a thing is to occur by chance. People are notoriously bad at evaluating probabilities, which is why casino owners make so much money. It is easy to over-estimate coincidences. How easy to say, 'Every time I think about my mother, she calls', and yet if you think about her a lot and she calls every day, then there is no coincidence here at all. In estimating risk, people believe that some rare event, such as a plane crash, is a greater risk than more commonplace events such as driving a car, and yet commercial air travel is six times safer per mile than auto travel. People commonly ascribe almost no risk to actions over which they believe they have some control, such as riding a bike or driving a car.

With such demonstrated poor judgement at evaluating probabilities of rare events, even for events of ordinary experience, it is not surprising that people are very bad indeed at judging the validity of rare events of a mystical nature. What may be helpful here is to apply what we know from the science of probability. Given a known domain within which an event may occur, we can estimate how probable this event is in relation to the universe of all such possible events. For example, there are only two ways that a tossed coin may come up, heads or tails. We can thus assign a probability to a toss coming up heads as 0.5. In the case of more complex events, such as the probability that a person will get brain cancer, we base our calculations on survey data or medical records which give an overall incidence of this disease for the population as a whole.

Probability may also usefully be applied to the study of prophecy. One of the difficulties with prophecy is that establishing the domain in order to estimate a probability can be problematic. This is particularly so for very symbolic and veiled prophecies, such as those of Nostradamus, which can be interpreted any way one chooses. On the other hand, many prophecies once quantified may turn out to not have much predictive value. For example, if a prophecy says that there will be wars, or an earthquake or a meteor shower, it is easy to obtain historical frequencies of these types of events. We find that it is difficult to ascribe any particular war or earthquake or meteor shower to the given prophecy because almost any period in history would qualify as having these three types of disturbances. Of course, it is well to remember that when such physical events are described they may actually stand for spiritual realities, as described by 'Abdu'l-Bahá (above).

Calculating specific probabilities for these predicted events helps indicate their likelihood. Wars, dramatic meteors or comets and major earthquakes all have nearly a probability of 1.0 of occurring during any given lifetime. The chance of all three occurring together in some period of a few decades is their joint probability (obtained by multiplying) which is still near 1.0. Thus prophecies concerning such events, as in the Olivet discourse of Jesus,[3] do not have much predictive power because they are fulfilled repeatedly over time and thus probably act more as general warnings and refer to spiritual realities rather than to historical events.

A very unlikely and precisely specified event that is predicted and which nevertheless occurs, on the other hand, is a very strong proof. Such is the case in science when new phenomena or particles that have been predicted are actually found. When such predictions involve the seemingly impossible, such as Dirac's prediction of anti-matter (the positron), the success is even more remarkable.

The Bahá'í view is that a remarkable series of prophecies was simultaneously fulfilled at the coming of the Báb and Bahá'u'lláh. These twin Manifestations claim to be the specific fulfilment of the age of prophecy that began with Adam. A chief characteristic of this age or era has been the repeated warnings, visions, prophecies and promises of a great day to come, made by both major and minor Prophets of all the extant religious traditions. While many of these prophecies have been vague, quite a few of them have been rather specific. Given that we can clearly see whether specific prophecies have been fulfilled, it would be helpful to be able to assess the probabilities that these events deviate from a chance expectation.

It is useful to illustrate the proposed approach with

an example. Shortly before His martyrdom, Jesus spoke to His disciples concerning the signs which would accompany His return. He gave a series of symbolic signs such as the sun not giving its light and the stars falling from heaven as well as general warning signs such as wars and rumours of wars. The import of these signs is given by Sours.[4] Jesus also gave a series of specific signs referring to real world events. He stated that when all these events came to pass, then and only then would He return in the station of the Father and in great glory. One of these signs was the destruction of Jerusalem by the Romans and the scattering of the Jews, both of which occurred shortly after His death. Three other specific prophecies concern us here: that His message would be preached in all the world, that the times of the Gentiles would be fulfilled and that the period of 2,300 years of Daniel would be completed. The first prophecy has a clear meaning: He would not return (that is, the Comforter would not come) until His message had been spread to the entire world. This event may be said to have occurred some time in the mid-1800s when European explorers and missionaries finally penetrated the interiors of Africa and South America.[5] For the second two prophecies He referred His listeners to Daniel concerning the abomination of desolation (or abomination which makes desolate), which is the period during which the holy temple in Jerusalem would be desecrated by non-Jews, or some event symbolically similar to this. Daniel gives two signs for this time. One is a period of years which is easily calculated to end in 1844,[6] and the other is the actual return of the Jews to

Israel. If the Jews had returned at any time before 1844 then the specific numerical prophecy of Daniel would have been invalidated. We may date the return of the Jews to Israel from 1844 with the Edict of Toleration, which the British government forced the Ottomans to sign and following which the Jews began to return to Palestine. They had been banned from this region from Roman times until then by a succession of ruling governments. We thus have three specific prophecies regarding dates when a new Manifestation is expected and which are fulfilled in the exact year in which the Báb declared His mission. While He could have possibly voluntarily fulfilled the date given by Daniel, fulfilment of the other two prophecies was certainly beyond His control.

Exactly how remarkable is the coincidental series of overlapping fulfilled prophecies? It is necessary in some way to assess the likelihood that these events could have occurred by chance without their occurrence having any significance, as in the examples of the comets and earthquakes above. Let us convert them to probabilities. We begin by noting that the period from Jesus' death to the present is about two thousand years. This is the period for fulfilment of these prophecies. The fulfilment of the 2,300 years of Daniel occurs in 1844.[7] The probability that the specific date of Daniel's prophecy should fall in that specific year in which the Bahá'í Faith began is 1/2000. The other two prophecies must overlap with this date to be valid. It is difficult to designate an exact year in when Jesus' message was preached in all the world, but it certainly occurred over the hundred-year span centred on 1844 because this was the period in which Christianity finally penetrated the remote corners of the world such as the Amazon basin and the heart of Africa. Let us be overly conservative and say that there is a hundred-year period that would qualify, which gives 100/2000 as the window for overlap of these events. The Edict of Toleration occurred in a specific year, 1844, so again we have a chance of 1/2000 that the Jews were able to begin to return in that particular year (fulfilling the times of the Gentiles) and not any other. The chance that all three of these events overlapped in time exactly is their product: (1/2000) × (100/2000) × (1/2000) which gives an overall chance of 1/80,000,000.

We may also attempt to estimate a probability for the chance that the Jews were able to return to Israel at all. In order to return, they first had to be dispersed, as predicted by Christ's first prophecy concerning the time of troubles which He said would come soon. It is not possible to give exact numbers for this, but we can estimate that there are roughly ten thousand 'peoples' on earth, where by this I mean a group larger than a village or clan, but no larger than a small nation. Of these perhaps five hundred have been totally banished from their original homes during historical times in the sense the Jews were (versus merely migrating as a unit some short distance away). As examples, we have the many tribes of American Indians, of Africans led to slavery, the gypsies, etc. Thus the chance that Christ's first prophecy (the dispersal) would come true is about 500/10,000 or 1/20. Of these cases, it is difficult to think of any besides the Jews who have

successfully returned to their homeland in historical
times. Some few American blacks attempted to
return to Africa, but their attempt to establish a state
was largely unsuccessful. Let us be generous and say
that there have been ten such returns out of the five
hundred. This gives a chance of 1/50. The overall
probability of a people first being banished and then
returning to the same homeland may thus be conserva-
tively estimated at $(1/50) \times (1/20) = 1/1000$. We must
combine this probability with that calculated above
to get an overall probability for this fulfilment. This
gives us $(1/80,000,000) \times (1/1000) = 1/80,000,000,000$
(one out of 80 billion).

There is one further very specific prophecy which
we may relate to this date. As mentioned above, the
prophecy of Daniel gives the date of 2,300 years
(spoken of symbolically as 2,300 days) from the
rebuilding of the temple until the time of the end. In
addition to these dates, Daniel gives a period of 1,260
days (years) as being important. Earlier Christian
attempts to find a significance for this period of time
involved various starting dates important in Christian
or Jewish history, but as nothing of consequence
could be attributed to the period of 1,260 years
following these dates, there was some disillusion-
ment with Daniel's prophecies.[8] After all, if only
some of his prophecies were correct, then maybe the
ones that were correct were mere coincidences. The
Bahá'í assertion that Bahá'u'lláh is the promised one
of all religions, however, allows us to expand our
search. We then see that the year 1260 is given some
importance in Islam. The Islamic calendar begins on
the date Muḥammad was forced to flee from Mecca

to Medina. In this lunar calendar, based on a slightly shorter year of 12 months of 30 days each, the year 1260 comes out to 1844 in the western calendar. Note that Muḥammad did not pick a new date that would conveniently come out to 1844 and speak of this date in his prophecy; rather the period of 1,260 years already existed in the Old Testament independently of Islam and the starting point for evaluating this prophecy is the very starting point for Islam. Muḥammad warned His followers to beware of the year 1260. Thus the coincidence of these dates in the fulfilment of Daniel's prophecy is truly remarkable.

How do we estimate a probability for this? This period of 1,260 days (years) refers to the abomination of desolation (or oppression that makes desolate).[9] The Bahá'í interpretation is that this refers to the usurpation of the faith of Islam by the Umayyid dynasty which caused untold harm to Islam.[10] The insinuation of the Umayyids into Islam began at the religion's very inception, thus the 1,260 years may date from the beginning of the Islamic calendar. Many Christian scholars also interpreted this abomination of desolation as referring not to an idol being set up in Jerusalem by the ungodly, but to a corruption of the true religion in some way. The various dates proposed by Christian scholars over the centuries as being the beginning of such a devastating event include various heresies, civil wars among Christians, the corruption of the Papacy, the exile of the Jews and other events of this type. We could say that there are perhaps a hundred such major events over the last two thousand years (to be very generous). Only one, the beginning of the

Islamic calendar, has an ending date that corresponds to any historical cleansing or renewal process: that of the beginning of the Bahá'í Faith in 1844. Thus we have a probability of 100/2000 or 1/20 that this date is a coincidence (there are one hundred chances that during the last two thousand years an event would occur which would match the prophecy). Combining this with the previous calculation, we have (1/20) × (1/80,000,000,000) which gives 1/1,600,000,000,000 (one out of 1.6 trillion) as the chance that all of these events occurred simultaneously purely by coincidence. Note also that not only do we observe that all of these things occurred, but that they represent the complete fulfilment of all the specific predictions of both Jesus and Daniel. Even if we factor out one of these dates (the periods of 1,260 or 2,300 years) by assuming that the founders of the Bahá'í Faith had read the prophecy and voluntarily set out to fulfil it, we still get the chance of the remaining overlapping coincidences as 1/800,000,000 (by multiplying by 2,000 for the fulfilment of the 2,300 years) or one out of 800 million. Alternatively, we can factor out the 1,260 years as being a date picked for fulfilment, but that leaves the others as still being unexplained with a one out of 80 billion chance.

The probability calculated above is a remarkably small number, far too small to attribute the simultaneous fulfilment of these prophecies to chance. We note that in science we are satisfied if the probability of getting a particular result by chance is less than 1/100. We may get a feel for the real improbability of a one out of 80 billion chance by imagining the following: somewhere in the Amazon jungle there is an ant with a small mark of paint placed on it. You are dropped at random out into the jungle and must bend down and pick up one ant. That ant turns out to be the correct ant with the mark on it. If proving the correctness of all the holy books of the past depended on such an unlikely event, one might not have much hope of such a proof, but in fact that is how unlikely it is that these several independent prophecies were all fulfilled simultaneously, along with others, with the coming of the Báb and Bahá'u'lláh.

Thus the year 1844 appears to be the specific year promised by Jesus for His return in the glory of the Father, measured both in terms of specific dates and worldly events. For the literal minded, we note that the world did not end in that year. Of course, this is not a complete proof of the divine origin of the Báb's message, but it certainly does point to 1844 as being a remarkable year which bears closer examination. We may use a similar approach to assess other prophecies such as the places Bahá'u'lláh was sent as an exile and certain events that took place. For example, there are explicit Old Testament prophecies that 'in that day' the Lord would come from Elam (Persia), and that the Lord would establish His house on Mount Carmel in the vicinity of the Plain of Sharon and 'Akká, and that the new Prophet would walk by the banks of the Tigris river near what is now Baghdad. Muḥammad praised 'Akká highly and hinted at its future special station using terms He did not use for any other place. This is a set of specific prophecies not framed in symbolic language and all of which were fulfilled by Bahá'u'lláh.[11] Bahá'u'lláh was born in Elam (Persia), spent ten years on the banks of the Tigris at Baghdad as an exile, and was sent to 'Akká, near Mount Carmel and the Plain of Sharon, again as an exile. When we examine these further very specific prophecies in the light of whether they occurred by chance, we heap improbabilities upon improbabilities, finally reaching the conclusion that it is impossible that these events are a coincidence. If rational proof were sufficient, then there would be no room for doubt. In the realm of religion, of course, rational proof is not the ultimate criterion, but it is interesting that in this day, when science is supreme, we have been given such convincing and logical signs. It is most appropriate.

9

God Under the Microscope

For the last few hundred years we have looked for God under our microscopes and, failing to find Him there, have concluded that He does not exist. I would like to suggest that we have been looking in the wrong places, asking the wrong questions and demanding the wrong evidence. Science does show that a corporeal God sitting on a throne just above the clouds is a nonsensical concept, but true religious faith is not contingent on belief in such a God in any case. The fact that science has not found Him with the microscope or telescope is not terribly surprising, but is not really much of a proof either. Nor does the arbitrary assertion that the concept of God is 'illogical' from a scientific standpoint carry much weight because, for example, the very fact that we exist is itself rather illogical. *A priori* plausibility is not a very strong argument. Thus it is clear that these issues need a more detailed and thoughtful treatment. I begin by examining in more detail the major arguments offered by science against God's existence. Following this I present a new framework for evidence and three specific lines of argument: predictive power, theory coherence and consilience of different lines of evidence.

Traditional Arguments and the Nature of Evidence

One of the strongest arguments against God's existence has been the difficulties posed by assuming that the Bible is literally true. There are many events in the Bible which contradict scientific laws and evidence, such as the stories of Jonah and Noah. It has been argued that if the Bible is God's word (hypothesis), and the events in it if taken literally could not have happened (test of hypothesis), then God does not exist (inference). Notice the key 'if' here: 'if taken literally'. This 'if' is taken as mandatory by fundamentalists who fear that taking one thing as metaphorical will open the door to unbounded doubt about the whole thing. The Bahá'í view is that literalness is not a prerequisite of faith. The metaphorical nature of many Bible stories is explained (see *The Book of Certitude* and *Some Answered Questions*) and it is asserted that all of these stories contain important truths. It is not necessary for the stories to be taken literally for us to learn from them, to be uplifted by them and to be reborn. For example, the story of Noah concerns the great metaphor of the ark, which stands for the safety to be found only in God's Word and His Law. The story of Jonah concerns steadfastness under adversity. It is not a disparagement of the Bible to note that it contains many metaphors because metaphors and stories are the best medium to reach diverse and largely uneducated peoples, as Christianity did in its spread across the globe (see chapter on 'Entropy' in this volume). Metaphors are also more easily translated into diverse languages. Furthermore, those specific statements made in the Bible which have a direct bearing on science (the creation story, the flood, the chronology of descendants of Adam, etc.) are specifically mentioned in the Bahá'í writings as being metaphorical so that there would be no doubt about the issue (see chapter on 'Evolution' in this volume). Thus the difficulties caused by literal interpretation of metaphors do not exist in the Bahá'í Faith.

A second traditional argument against God's existence concerns the existence of evil. The argument is as follows: If God is all-knowing and all-powerful and evil exists, then God has knowingly permitted it to exist even though He could prevent it, which either means that God is evil (a contradiction) or that He does not exist. The Bahá'í writings resolve this dilemma. As discussed by Hatcher,[1] the Bahá'í view is that evil is a necessary consequence of the existence of free will. In a world in which all evil, pain and hardship were prevented by God, no one would have a choice to be either good or evil; all would be predetermined. Being good in such a world would not reflect an ethical choice but would be involuntary. Only voluntary choices can be rewarded as being good or moral. But to allow choice also allows evil to occur. Thus free will and the existence of evil are the two sides of one coin. Hatcher[2] presents a beautiful treatment of this idea using the tools of formal logic. Thus the existence of evil is not a proof that God is uncaring or evil or nonexistent.

The final major scientific argument against God's existence concerns the apparent lack of evidence for Him. Scientists say that if He existed we would have seen Him by now. However, the type of evidence being sought is not even the type which science itself is asked to produce. We cannot see God in our microscopes but gravity is not visible in a microscope either. There are many scientific realities which are impervious to the senses. We are only able to detect them by some effect that they produce. No one has yet seen an atom. We detect atoms by photographing the pertubations they cause as they pass through a bubble chamber or some other device. The existence of electromagnetic waves travelling through the air cannot be guessed merely by looking around, but if one turns on a radio then music can be heard. Without an instrument to detect an effect, we remain without knowledge of these invisible forces and properties. The fact that we cannot detect radio waves unassisted does not disprove their existence. We may make an analogy here and say that the Manifestations of God are like the radio receivers for the divine spirit. The fact that most of us are not such receivers does not disprove the reality of that spirit. Likewise, if we now and again pick up a hint of the divine spirit ourselves, this does not mean that we have a direct line to God any more than the person who picks up some music on his dental braces is really a radio.

This basic scientific principle that many realities are invisible and must be studied by their effects or properties is also reflected in the Bahá'í teachings. 'Abdu'l-Bahá explains:

As our knowledge of things, even of created and
limited things, is knowledge of their qualities and not
of their essence, how is it possible to comprehend in
its essence the Divine Reality, which is unlimited?
For the substance of the essence of anything is not
comprehended, but only its qualities. For example,
the substance of the sun is unknown, but is understood by its qualities, which are heat and light. The
substance of the essence of man is unknown and not
evident, but by its qualities it is characterized and
known. Thus everything is known by its qualities and
not by its essence.[3]

Thus we should not expect to detect God's essence
any more than we expect to see a cup full of gravity.
Rather, we should be looking for effects in the
external world by which we may infer that some
hidden force is at work. If the Manifestations of God
are that instrument by which the invisible is made
visible in the realm of the spirit, then it is to them
that we should turn for evidence.

   This, then, is our first type of evidence: examination of the lives and teachings of the Prophets.
Failure to use this type of evidence may be compared
to the church leaders who would not look through
Galileo's telescope. When we study the Prophets, we
see that all of them arose in obscure places, not in
the centres of power and learning. Each was devoid
of formal education and was without worldly power;
and yet each caused a change in the culture, morals
and behaviour of society for centuries following His
death. Not one of them ever trained as a priest or a
scholar. Even Bahá'u'lláh, who was of noble lineage,
was only taught such skills as poetry, calligraphy and

horsemanship. One of the remarkable feats, which we may observe in both the Báb and Bahá'u'lláh, is the power of their revelational writings. When these two Manifestations were moved by the Divine Spirit, they would spontaneously dictate prayers or compositions in finished form, perfect in every way. For example, Bahá'u'lláh revealed *The Book of Certitude* in two days of continuous dictation to His secretary. The Báb revealed thousands of verses at a time in front of His listeners in response to questions, spontaneously and without stopping. To anyone who has ever written something complex, the idea that an entire book can be revealed at one sitting and without alteration is simply unfathomable. Evidence such as the above seems to support the conclusion that there is something extraordinary about these personages and their claim to be in receipt of a revelation from a higher power. We may, therefore, be justified in lending credence to their claims, thereby supporting the idea that God exists.

New Arguments for God's Existence

Having disposed of traditional arguments against God's existence, and having presented the case for the types of evidence that are likely to be valid and useful, I next present some new arguments in favour of His existence.

Predictive Power

In the case of scientific theories, one of the strongest tests of their validity is the ability to predict some phenomenon.[4] For example, the quantum theory of the atom predicted the specific spectral lines found in light from various sources. If there were some such predictions made in the context of religion, then this would be a strong test of the truth of the claim that religion is divinely inspired rather than man-made. We do in fact have this situation in the form of the prophecies made and fulfilled by each of the Prophets. How such prophecies can be made is impossible to understand fully. Nevertheless, we have a set of observable, testable predictions which we may examine. Appropriately enough for this scientific age, the Bahá'í dispensation has been accompanied by the fulfilment of past prophecies so specific, numerous and varied that the idea that these are coincidences is not tenable. For example, in the chapter 'Probability and Prophecy' we saw that the statements of Jesus to His disciples concerning the conditions which must be met before His return revolve around the exile and return of the Jews to Israel and specify the year 1844. The chance that all of His prophetic utterances would be fulfilled simultaneously on and around 1844 was shown to be approximately one in 80 billion. We also note that Bahá'u'lláh made prophecies about the fates of the kings of the major empires of His day, such as Tsarist Russia and the Ottoman empire, empires and kingdoms which had stood for over five hundred years in many instances. In every case, when Bahá'u'lláh pronounced to a ruler that his kingdom would soon fall, that kingdom not only fell but was shattered, the royal line obliterated and sometimes even the name of the country was changed. The one royal household, that of England, which He favoured with a positive Tablet is the only one of that group still reigning. There are many other examples of this type. If a series of prophecies is made which seems impossible of fulfilment but are nevertheless met, one by one, inclusively, then it would seem that the most severe test of science, predictive power, has been met. Again, since the ones making and fulfilling these prophecies claim to represent a higher power, these results tend to support their claims and support God's existence.

Theory Coherence

Theory coherence is a second major test of a scientific theory. If the parts of a theory conflict with one another, it is clear that something is wrong. In the practice of science this property is often evaluated to see if a theory is incomplete, is too vague or is wrong by seeing if divergent predictions can be derived from it. For example, in ecology, Optimal Foraging Theory makes predictions about how animals should behave with respect to finding food. One prediction derived from this theory was that in a time of food scarcity animals should become desperate and try to catch anything that moves rather than just their usual preferred prey. Another aspect of the theory predicted that competition should produce specialists. This contradiction was bothersome until it was realized that the second prediction concerns changes over long time periods owing to evolution, thus resolving the contradiction. The hollow earth theory is an example of an internally conflicting theory, one which violates many laws of physics as well as being self-contradictory. In addition to contradictions, a theory may be *ad hoc*, consisting of a collection of assertions with no necessary relation to each other. Such a theory is incoherent. As an example of an incoherent theory, we might cite New Age philosophy which promotes healing crystals, past lives, UFOs and astrology. There is no necessary connection among any of these elements. Any one of them could be replaced by its opposite (no UFOs) without affecting the rest of the philosophy. This shows that this theory does not hang together.

Applying this criteron of truth to religion in the case of the Bahá'í Faith yields some very interesting results. We may first note coherence with respect to external reality. There are no major tenets of the Bahá'í Faith in conflict with science, even on issues such as evolution (see chapter on 'Evolution' in this volume). Miracles also do not pose a problem. Bahá'u'lláh denies that miracles violate the laws of nature. The miracles involved in the Bahá'í dispensation are more on the order of divine coincidences. For example, the entire firing squad (some 750 men) which executed the Báb met an untimely end. Part of the squad was involved in a rebellion and was executed in the very same way as the Báb. The rest were asleep in the shade of a long wall when an earthquake caused it to collapse on them, killing them all. There are many examples of this type, where we can see the divine hand at work but where no physical laws are broken. It was also noted above that biblical literalness does not present a problem with respect to contradicting physical laws because strict literalness is not insisted upon. Thus we may recognize coherence with respect to external reality.

A second aspect of coherence involves internal coherence. For example, in atomic theory there are many component parts of the theory which interact in multiple ways with respect to different phenomena, demonstrating that the different components are compatible and fit together. We find a remarkable internal coherence in the Bahá'í revelation, in epistemology, theology, metaphysics and social teachings. For example, the promise that this is the day of the achievement of world peace is made concrete by the presentation of a set of teachings which attack the root causes of war. The teachings given to bring about peace, such as the elimination of prejudice and the equality of men and women, are consistent with other primary aspects of the Faith and mutually reinforce each other. This internal coherence accounts for the lack of anxiety Bahá'ís evince when confronted with difficult questions. It has often been noted by those attending Bahá'í meetings that there is a certitude, a calmness, even in the face of very difficult questions, that differs from the certitude of the fanatic, and this in spite of the fact that there are no clergy to act as experts. This certitude comes from the long experience of Bahá'ís that the teachings of their Faith all fit together logically and convincingly. There are no sensitive topics which must be avoided, nor is their faith based on an unprovable miracle such as the physical resurrection.

A third and remarkable type of coherence involves the resolutions of contradictions in past religious teachings. For example, in one place Jesus says, 'before Abraham was, I am', in which He seems to equate Himself with God; and yet in another place He says that He does only what His Father shows Him and that the Father knows things which the Son knows not. This seems to be a serious confusion over His essential nature. Bahá'u'lláh explains that the Prophets have three stations, that of a man, that of a Prophet and that of the direct mouthpiece of God Himself. They speak at different times in different voices. Thus in the example above, Christ spoke at one time as a Prophet and at another as God Himself. This explanation clarifies an apparent internal contradiction in Christianity and lends more credence to the story of Jesus. A similar explanation of the meaning of the story of Adam and Eve resolves the inconsistent conclusions that have resulted from this story.[5] For example, if God is all-knowing, then He knew that Adam and Eve would disobey and eat the fruit, and therefore punishing them and their descendants was a cruel trick. Alternatively, we may view it as a metaphor on the existence of free will. We are all faced with the choice to obey or disobey God, to choose material or spiritual realities. We have all eaten of the fruit of the tree of the knowledge of good and evil, and thereby been banned from the innocent world inhabited by the animals. But this is not an on-going punishment for an inevitable act (original sin); rather it is a consequence of the fact that we have free choice and must therefore choose. Many other contradictions existing in past religious teachings are also resolved in this way, reflecting the encompassing coherence evident in the Bahá'í teachings. As Bahá'u'lláh says, 'We have unsealed the choice Wine with the fingers of might and power.'[6] He also notes that this is the day in which the books of God are unsealed.

Thus we may say that the Bahá'í Faith exhibits notable external, internal and retrodictive coherence. If we have a scientific theory, one of whose postulates is difficult to test directly, then we often rely for our assessment on the overall performance of the theory. In this case, the high degree of coherence of the theory (the religious teachings) leads us to have confidence in the parts of the theory (God's existence) that we cannot test directly.

Consilience *diverse lines of evidence all point to same conclusion*

When it is impossible to conduct an experiment upon a subject, we look for existing evidence which we may evaluate. For example, we can not create a sun in the laboratory, so we study the light from the sun and compare it to other suns. We can not go back and observe the ice ages or the extinction of the dinosaurs, so we are forced to weigh various threads of evidence, none of which is convincing by itself. When diverse lines of existence all point to the same conclusion, however, this is called consilience. A term for the procedure of comparing diverse items of evidence is meta-analysis. Meta-analysis is a useful tool to apply to the question of God's existence. By this method we may combine various sources of weak evidence in order to come to a stronger conclusion.

We may now place our previous arguments in this

context. We showed that the scientific arguments against God's existence are dispelled by the Bahá'í teachings. Disproving a negative argument does not prove its opposite, but it does move the event from the impossible to the possible (though not necessarily to the probable) realm. There are a number of other arguments, however, which we may examine and combine.

First we note the three arguments made for God's existence above: the evidence of the persons of the Manifestations and their lives; the predictive power argument based on the fulfilment of prophecy and retrodictive explanation of anomalies in past theology; and the argument of theory coherence. Together these three lines of evidence appear quite strong. Let us examine some further arguments.

One of the classic arguments for God's existence is the argument from design. If we look at a watch, we observe that it is highly ordered, complex and performs a function, being thus highly unlikely to be the result of chance events. We thus conclude that there must be a watchmaker. By this same line of argument we observe a complex and well-ordered natural world and conclude from this that there is a God. 'Abdu'l-Bahá makes this argument in detail in a letter to Dr August Forel.[7] This argument does seem persuasive but is not airtight because we are left wondering who then created God. Nevertheless, this may be considered to be a positive argument, even if not very strong.

Another argument for God's existence is that without Him and without humanity to know and worship Him, then existence would be totally void and without meaning.[8] While it is not possible to prove that meaningfulness is a necessary property of existence, the fact that the universe is structured just perfectly for human life to exist and coincides with the abstractions of mathematics so well suggests the possibility that this argument has some weight. Again this argument is not a strong one, but points in the same direction.

An ancient argument, dating back to Aristotle, is that it is not possible to have an infinite regress of causation. That is, as we trace back the chain of causation in the world, there must at some point be an uncaused cause or first cause, which we may call God. Again, there are flaws in this argument (the first cause might not necessarily be a sentient being or might no longer be operative) but there is some plausibility in it.[9]

A final argument concerns the mystical experience. Throughout history and in every culture individuals have had mystical experiences in which they feel certain that they have contacted some essence, power, intelligence or spirit. Such subjective experiences are notoriously difficult to verify. The variety of these experiences suggests that whatever ability the average person has to make such contact is imperfect at best. This in fact is why Bahá'ís believe that the Manifestations of God are needed, to be a clear channel for God's word. The ubiquity of this phenomenon and the intensity of the experiences to those who have them suggest the possibility that something real is taking place. This again points to God's existence.

Overall, then, there are a variety of lines of

evidence and logical arguments, all of which point to the same conclusion: some type of real spiritual phenomenon exists in the world which appears to be directed or generated by an unseen power which we call God. No single argument or piece of evidence is conclusive, but all lines of argument either fail to disprove Him or point to His existence.

Conclusion

The search for God will never be successful as long as we look for the wrong type of evidence and make *a priori* conclusions about His existence being illogical. Not even gravity can be detected by merely looking around, nor can it be photographed or held in a cup; we should not expect God to be. To detect a force or property we must look at the appropriate domain where that force or property is manifested. Thus it is necessary that we examine the phenomenon of religion itself as the domain where God manifests Himself, and the Prophets of God in particular as the recipients of His power. When we do this, we find various lines of evidence, many of them very powerful, others less so, but all pointing in the same direction: there is an unobservable essence called God and the Prophets are His messengers.

Bibliography

'Abdu'l-Bahá. *Selections from the Writings of 'Abdu'l-Bahá*. Translated by a Committee at the Bahá'í World Centre and by Marzieh Gail. Haifa: Bahá'í World Centre, 1978.

——*Some Answered Questions*. Translated by Laura Clifford Barney. Wilmette, Illinois: Bahá'í Publishing Trust, 2nd edn., 1981.

Bahá'u'lláh. *Epistle to the Son of the Wolf*. Wilmette, Illinois: Bahá'í Publishing Trust, 1988.

——*Gleanings from the Writings of Bahá'u'lláh*. Wilmette, Illinois: Bahá'í Publishing Trust, 1983.

——*The Hidden Words*. Wilmette, Illinois: Bahá'í Publishing Trust, 1990.

——*The Kitáb-i-Íqán* (*The Book of Certitude*). Wilmette, Illinois: Bahá'í Publishing Trust, 1989.

——*Prayers and Meditations*. Wilmette, Illinois: Bahá'í Publishing Trust, 1987.

——*The Seven Valleys and the Four Valleys*. Translated by Marzieh Gail. Wilmette, Illinois: Bahá'í Publishing Trust, 1991.

——*Tablets of Bahá'u'lláh revealed after the Kitáb-i-Aqdas*. Compiled by the Research Department of the Universal House of Justice and translated by Habib Taherzadeh with the assistance of a Committee at the Bahá'í World Centre. Wilmette, Illinois: Bahá'í Publishing Trust, rev. edn. 1988.

Bahá'u'lláh and 'Abdu'l-Bahá. *Bahá'í World Faith*. Wilmette, Illinois: Bahá'í Publishing Trust, rev. edn. 1976.

——*The Reality of Man*. Wilmette, Illinois: Bahá'í Publishing Trust, 1966.

Balyuzi, H. M. *Bahá'u'lláh, the King of Glory*. Oxford: George Ronald, 1980.

Bloom, A. *The Closing of the American Mind*. New York: Simon and Schuster, 1987.

Boorstin, D. J. *The Discoverers*. New York: Random House, 1983.

Boxer, S. 'Will Creationism Rise Again?' *Discover* 8 (1987):80–5.

Burhoe, R. W. 'Natural Selection and God'. *Zygon* 7 (1976):30–63.

——'The Source of Civilization in the Natural Selection of Coadapted Information in Genes and Culture'. *Zygon* 11 (1976): 263–303.

Campbell, D. T. 'The Conflict between Social and Biological Evolution and the Concept of Original Sin'. *Zygon* 10 (1975):234–49.

——'On the Conflict between Biological and Social Evolution and between Psychology and Moral Tradition'. *Zygon* 11 (1976):167–208.

Conservation of the Earth's Resources. A compilation of extracts from the Bahá'í Writings prepared by the Research Department of the Universal House of Justice. London: Bahá'í Publishing Trust, 1990.

Dahl, Arthur Lyon. *Unless and Until: A Bahá'í Focus on the Environment*. Oakham: Bahá'í Publishing Trust, 1990.

Darwin, Charles. *The Formation of Vegetable Mould, through the Action of Worms, with Observations on their Habits*. London: John Murray, 1881.

——*The Structure and Distribution of Coral Reefs*. London: Smith and Elder, 1842.

Davis, B. D. 'Evolution, Human Diversity and Society'. *Zygon* 11 (1976):80–95.

Diamond, J. 'The Accidental Conqueror'. *Discover* Dec. 1989, pp. 71–6.

Dobzhansky, T., and Boesiger, E. *Human Culture: A Moment in Evolution.* ed. B Wallace. New York: Columbia University Press, 1983.

Fitzgerald, Michael. *The Creative Circle.* Los Angeles: Kalimat Press, 1989.

Futuyma, D. J. *Evolutionary Biology.* Sunderland, Massachusetts: Sinauer Associates, 1979.

Geist, V. *Life Strategies, Human Evolution, Environmental Design.* New York: Springer-Verlag, 1978.

Hatcher, William. *Logic and Logos: Essays on Science, Religion and Philosophy.* Oxford: George Ronald, 1990.

Hawking, Stephen. W. *A Brief History of Time.* New York: Bantam, 1988.

Hoagland, H. 'Reflections on the Purpose of Life'. *Zygon* 6 (1971):28–38.

Kaye, H. L. *The Social Meaning of Modern Biology.* New Haven: Yale University Press, 1986.

Khursheed, Anjam. *Science and Religion: Towards the Restoration of an Ancient Harmony.* Guernsey: One World Publications, 1987.

Koeslag, J. H. 'Koinophilia groups sexual creatures into species, promotes stasis, and stabilizes social behavior'. *Journal of Theoretical Biology* 144 (1990):15–35.

Kricher, J. C. Letter to the editor. *Bulletin of the Ecological Society of America.* 67 (1986):262.

——Letter to the editor. *Bulletin of the Ecological Society of America.* 68 (1987):487–8.

Lewin, R. 'Africa: Cradle of Modern Humans'. *Science.* 237 (1987):1292–5.

——'Modern Human Origins under Close Scrutiny'. *Science.* 239 (1988): 1240–1.

Loehle, Craig, 'Hypothesis Testing in Ecology: Psychological Aspects and the Importance of Theory Maturation'. *Quarterly Review of Biology.* 62 (1987):397–409.

——'Phototropism of whole trees: Effects of habitat and growth form'. *American Midland Naturalist.* 116 (1986):190–6.

——'Tree Life History Strategies: The Role of Defenses'. *Canadian Journal of Forest Research*. 18 (1988):209–22.

Margolis, H. *Patterns, Thinking, and Cognition*. Chicago: University of Chicago Press, 1987.

Mühlschlegel, Peter. *Auguste Forel and the Bahá'í Faith*. Oxford: George Ronald, 1978.

Murphy, E. J. *History of African Civilization*. New York: Thomas Y. Crowell Co., 1972.

Nabíl-i-A'zam. *The Dawn-Breakers: Nabíl's Narrative of the Early Days of the Bahá'í Revelation*. Translated by Shoghi Effendi. Wilmette, Illinois: Bahá'í Publishing Trust, 1962.

Oliver, J. D. 'Ecology and Creation'. *Bulletin of the Ecological Society of America*. 67 (1986):229–30.

Popper, Karl R. *Conjectures and Refutations: The Growth of Scientific Knowledge*. New York: Harper and Row, 1963.

——*The Logic of Scientific Discovery*. London: Hutchinson, 1959.

Rise, S. 'Creationist Ecology?' *Bulletin of the Ecological Society of America*. 67 (1986):8–10.

——Letter to the editor. *Bulletin of the Ecological Society of America*. 68 (1987):2–3.

Root-Bernstein, R. S. *Discovering*. Cambridge, Massachusetts: Harvard University Press, 1989.

Russell, D. 'A New Specimen of Stenonychosaurus from the Oldman Formation (Cretaceous) of Alberta.' *Canadian Journal of Earth Sciences*. 6 (1969):595–612.

Sears, William. *Thief in the Night*. Oxford: George Ronald, 1961.

Shapiro, A. M. 'God and Science'. *The Pennsylvania Gazette*, October 1987, pp. 47–51.

Shoghi Effendi. *The Advent of Divine Justice*. Wilmette, Illinois: Bahá'í Publishing Trust, 1990.

——*God Passes By*. Wilmette, Illinois: Bahá'í Publishing Trust, 1970.

——*The Promised Day is Come*. Wilmette, Illinois: Bahá'í Publishing Trust, rev. edn. 1980.

——*The World Order of Bahá'u'lláh*. Wilmette, Illinois: Bahá'í Publishing Trust, 1991.

Simmons, A. H., Kohler-Rollefson, I., Rollefson, G. O., Mandel, R. and Kafafi, Z. ' 'Ain Ghazal: A Major Neolithic Settlement in Central Jordan'. *Science*. 240 (1988):35–9.

Simonton, D. K. *Scientific Genius*. New York: Cambridge University Press, 1988.

Sours, Michael. *The Prophecies of Jesus*. Oxford: OneWorld, 1991.

Stein, G. J. 'Biological Science and the Roots of Nazism'. *American Scientist*. 76 (1988):50–8.

Strahler, A. N. *Science and Earth History: The Evolution/ Creation Controversy*. Buffalo, New York: Prometheus, 1987.

Stringer, C. B. 'The Dates of Eden'. *Nature* 331 (1988):565–6.

Stringer, C. B. and Andrews, P. 'Genetic and Fossil Evidence for the Origin of Modern Humans'. *Science* 239 (1988):1263–8.

Swartzman, D., and Rickard, L.J. 'Being Optimistic about the Search for Extraterrestrial Intelligence'. *American Scientist* 76 (1988):364–9.

Valladas, H., Reyss, J.L., Joron, J.L., Valladas, G., Bar-Yosef, O., and Vandermeersh, B. 'Thermoluminescence Dating of Mousterian "Proto-Cro-Magnon" Remains from Israel and the Origin of Modern Man'. *Nature*. 331 (1988):614–16.

Watson, D. *The Double Helix*. New York: New American Library, 1968.

Whimbey, A. and Whimbey, L. S. *Intelligence Can Be Taught*. New York: Bantam, 1976.

White, R. *Spiritual Foundations for an Ecologically Sustainable Society*. Montreal: Association for Bahá'í Studies, 1989.

Wilson, E. O. *Biophilia*. Cambridge: Harvard University Press, 1984.

Zuckerkandl, E. 'Creationism and Evolution'. *Nature*. 334 (1988): 376.

References

Introduction

1. Dan. 12:9.
2. John 16:12–13.

1. Race: A Combined Scientific and Spiritual Perspective

1. See Lewin, *Africa*.
2. See ibid.; Lewin, *Human Origins*; and Stringer and Andrews, 'Genetic and Fossil Evidence'.
3. See Lewin, *Africa* and *Human Origins*.
4. See Stringer and Andrews, 'Genetic and Fossil Evidence'.
5. ibid.
6. See Koeslag, 'Koinophilia'.
7. See Diamond, 'The Accidental Conqueror'.
8. See Murphy, *African Civilization*.
9. See Boorstin, *Discoverers*.
10. Shoghi Effendi, *Promised Day is Come*, pp. 113–14.
11. Bahá'u'lláh, *Hidden Words*, Arabic no. 68.
12. Reduced income and marriage chances shown for fat women and short men, Chicago *Sun Times*, 30 Sept. 1993.
13. 'Abdu'l-Bahá, cited in Shoghi Effendi, *Advent*, p. 37.
14. 'Abdu'l-Bahá, in *Bahá'í World Faith*, pp. 257–8.

2. Spiritual Synergy for a New Ecology

1. 'Abdu'l-Bahá, *Some Answered Questions*, pp. 3–4; see also chapter on 'Evolution' in this volume.
2. ibid. pp. 122–6.

3. Bahá'u'lláh, *Tablets*, p. 142.
4. Bahá'u'lláh, *Prayers and Meditations*, p. 272.
5. Bahá'u'lláh, *Epistle*, p. 44.
6. 'Abdu'l-Bahá, *Selections*, p. 275.
7. Bahá'u'lláh, *Hidden Words*, Persian no. 76.
8. Shoghi Effendi, cited in *Conservation*, p. 15.
9. See Dahl, *Unless and Until*.
10. See White, *Spiritual Foundations*.
11. According to a World Bank study, the education of women increases hygiene, reduces family size and aids economic development. Chicago *Sun Times*, 7 Sept. 1993.

3. Creativity: The Divine Gift

1. See Fitzgerald, *Creative Circle*.
2. See Simonton, *Scientific Genius*.
3. 'Abdu'l-Bahá, *Paris Talks*, pp. 41–2.
4. Bahá'u'lláh, *Gleanings*, p. 177.
5. Bahá'u'lláh, *Hidden Words*, Arabic no. 68.
6. See Loehle, 'Hypothesis Testing'.
7. See Margolis, *Patterns, Thinking and Cognition*.
8. See, for example, Darwin, *Coral Reefs*, and Darwin, *Vegetable Mould*.
9. Simonton, *Scientific Genius*.
10. Bahá'u'lláh, *Gleanings*, p. 261.
11. See Root-Bernstein, *Discovering*.
12. Watson, *Double Helix*.
13. See Whimbey and Whimbey, *Intelligence*.
14. See Loehle, 'Hypothesis Testing'.
15. See Root-Bernstein, *Discovering*.
16. 'Abdu'l-Bahá, *Selections*, pp. 144–5.
17. Bahá'u'lláh, *Gleanings*, p. 157.

4. Evolution in Bahá'í Perspective

1. Boorstin, *Discoverers*.
2. See, for example, Boxer, 'Creationism'; Kricher,

letters to editor of the *Bulletin of the Ecological Society of America*; Oliver, 'Ecology and Creation'; Rice, 'Creationist Ecology?'; Rice, letter to editor of the *Bulletin of the Ecological Society of America*; Shapiro, 'God and Science'; Strahler, *Controversy*, and Zuckerkandl, 'Creationism and Evolution'.

3. See Kaye, *Social Meaning*.
4. See Futuyma, *Evolutionary Biology*.
5. See Lewin, 'Africa'.
6. See ibid.; Lewin, 'Human Origins'; and Stringer and Andrews, 'Genetic and Fossil Evidence'.
7. See Lewin, 'Africa' and Lewin, 'Human Origins'.
8. See Stringer and Andrews, 'Genetic and Fossil Evidence'.
9. See Geist, *Life Strategies*.
10. See Simmons et al. 'Neolithic Settlement'.
11. See Burhoe, 'Source of Civilization'; and Dobzhansky and Boesiger, *Human Culture*.
12. See, for example, Burhoe, 'Natural Selection', and 'Source of Civilization'; Campbell, 'Conflict between Social and Biological Evolution'; and Davis, 'Evolution'.
13. See review in Kaye, *Social Meaning*.
14. Wilson, *Biophilia*.
15. See Stein, 'Nazism'.
16. ibid.
17. See Hawking, *Brief History of Time*.
18. Bahá'u'lláh, *Tablets*, pp. 140.
19. 'Abdu'l-Bahá, *Some Answered Questions*, pp. 183–4, 196–7.
20. Bahá'u'lláh. *Gleanings*, p. 163.
21. ibid.
22. See Swartzman and Rickard, 'Extraterrestrial Intelligence'.
23. 'Abdu'l-Bahá, *Some Answered Questions*, pp. 180–4.
24. 'Abdu'l-Bahá, in *Bahá'í World Faith*, p. 342.
25. ibid.

26. Bahá'u'lláh, *Gleanings*, p. 133.
27. 'Abdu'l-Bahá, *Some Answered Questions*, p. 244.
28. ibid. pp. 248–50. See also Hatcher, *Logic and Logos*.
29. 'Abdu'l-Bahá, *Some Answered Questions*, p. 248.
30. ibid. pp. 196–7.
31. See Dobzhansky and Boesiger, *Human Culture*.
32. 'Abdu'l-Bahá, *Some Answered Questions*, p. 199.
33. 'Abdu'l-Bahá, cited in Khursheed, *Science and Religion*.
34. 'Abdu'l-Bahá, *Some Answered Questions*, pp. 182–3.
35. ibid. pp. 193–4.
36. ibid. pp. 196–7.
37. See Swartzman and Rickard, 'Extraterrestrial Intelligence'.
38. Russell, 'New Specimen'.
39. 'Abdu'l-Bahá, *Some Answered Questions*, pp. 248–50.
40. ibid. pp. 191–4.
41. 'Abdu'l-Bahá, *Paris Talks*, p. 41.

5. Knowledge and Faith

1. 'Abdu'l-Bahá, *Some Answered Questions*, p. 220.
2. Bahá'u'lláh, *Kitáb-i-Íqán*, pp. 98–9.
3. 'Abdu'l-Bahá, *Some Answered Questions*, pp. 113–14.

6. Growth and Stability of the Bahá'í Administrative Order: Lessons from Biology

1. For a detailed treatment of these aspects of tree growth see Loehle, 'Tree Life History'.
2. Loehle, 'Phototropism'.

7. Entropy and the Integrity of the Sacred Texts

1. 'Abdu'l-Bahá, *Some Answered Questions*, p. 84.
2. Bahá'u'lláh, *Gleanings*, p. 318.
3. ibid. p. 264.
4. Nabíl-i-A'zam, *Dawn-Breakers*, pp. 631–2.

5. Bahá'u'lláh quoted in Shoghi Effendi, *God Passes By*, pp. 101–2.
6. ibid. pp. 222–3.
7. Bahá'u'lláh, *Seven Valleys*, pp. 4–5.

8. Probability and Prophecy

1. 'Abdu'l-Bahá, *Some Answered Questions*, pp. 84–5.
2. ibid. p. 111.
3. See Sours, *Prophecies of Jesus*.
4. ibid.
5. See Sears, *Thief*.
6. See Sours, *Prophecies of Jesus*.
7. See Sours, *Prophecies of Jesus*, and Sears, *Thief*, for detailed calculations.
8. See Sours, *Prophecies of Jesus*.
9. ibid.
10. ibid.
11. See Sears, *Thief*.

9. God Under the Microscope

1. See Hatcher, *Logic and Logos*.
2. ibid.
3. 'Abdu'l-Bahá, in *Bahá'í World Faith*, p. 321.
4. See Popper, *Scientific Discovery*, and *Scientific Knowledge*.
5. See 'Abdu'l-Bahá, *Some Answered Questions*, pp. 122–6.
6. Bahá'u'lláh, *Gleanings*, p. 332.
7. See Mühlschlegel, *Auguste Forel*.
8. See 'Abdu'l-Bahá, *Some Answered Questions*, pp. 177–9.
9. See Hatcher, *Logic and Logos*.